Swabbed
&FOUND

DISCLAIMER: Names and identifying circumstances have been changed to protect the privacy of those involved in this story. The author and publisher make no claims that readers would have similar DNA or ancestry search results as depicted in this memoir.

bright sky publishing
HOUSTON, TEXAS

2365 Rice Blvd., Suite 202
Houston, Texas 77005

ISBN: 978-1-942945-47-5

10   9   8   7   6   5   4

Library of Congress Cataloging-in-Publication Data on file with the publisher.

Editorial Director: Lauren Gow
Editor: Lucy Herring Chambers
Editor: Chuck Sambuchino
Editor: Melanie Saxton
Designer: Marla Y. Garcia

Printed in Canada through Friesens

For Beverly —
Enjoy...
Frank Billingsley

Swabbed
&FOUND

AN ADOPTED MAN'S DNA JOURNEY
TO DISCOVER HIS FAMILY TREE

FRANK BILLINGSLEY

bright sky publishing
HOUSTON, TEXAS

For Beverly –

Enjoy

[signature]

This book is dedicated to my family:
All 17,538 of you whom I have found so far.
Not to worry, I changed all your names.

Table of Contents

INTRODUCTION

We all want to know our family tree. We want to climb through its branches and find interesting characters who share traits just like ours. We want to discover where our big blue eyes came from, or our outgoing personality. We also wonder about what the branches of distant cousins and unknown ancestors might hold. We want to be proud of their heroic exploits, or we worry there might be something darker we need to know. Mainly, we want to discover who dealt us the genetic hand of cards we're playing.

For those of us who are adopted, the desire to understand the people whose DNA we share is even stronger. Yes, we have a family, and, yes, we may feel loved, but behind the family we know is the shadow of another family tree. Stories about people searching for family fascinate us. We cheer with Little Orphan Annie on Broadway as she finds her family and shiver with Luke Skywalker when he hears the harsh whisper, "I am your father." Sometimes when we search, the family we find is not what we had hoped.

Wondering about biological family can bring up fear: What if we don't like what we discover? Or, worse, what if we destroy what we already know?

Growing up in the South as the golden boy in my family, I always knew I was adopted. My mother made sure I understood that not only was I loved by the parents I knew, but also that I would have been loved by the birth parents I didn't know—if circumstances had been different. Now, I understand that she made that up, because she had no idea who they were. But her assurances of what a great athlete my birth father was and how pretty and smart my birth mother was did the trick. That little bit of a story kept me from wondering, too much. For years, I didn't admit I wanted to know about my birth parents, because I didn't want to hurt the parents I loved so much.

But, it simmered. There were mundane things, like health forms asking about family diseases. And awkward times, when people would say, "Oh you look just like your Mom," and I wondered if they were blind. Through all this, the need to know who was responsible for my own Big Bang, my personal DNA miracle, swirled inside.

At one point I played with the idea of searching for my biological parents, but I learned that the hospital with my birth records burned down. I took it as a sign that I was better off not knowing. It seemed like a relief at the time—I would never need to learn that I was descended from a long line of cattle rustlers, or worse. Besides, I was my folks' pride and joy and wanting to know any other parents other than them almost felt like cheating. They had never hurt me. I would never hurt them. I wrapped my genetic identity in Mom's little story about my pretty mother and athletic father, and I imagined any desire to know more went up in flames. I moved forward in my own life.

Deep down, it was a fifty-year-old lie. Of *course* I wanted to know who my birth parents were. I wanted to know where my love of theater came from, and my desire to debate and argue. Why am I bad with numbers but good with words? My adoptive mother made sure I never met a stranger, but what in me took that habit to the stage, when Mom fears reading the Bible out loud in Sunday school? On the upside, I had blue eyes and soft dirty-blonde hair—but who could I blame for a singing voice that had as much tone as a bus leaving the bus stop? I was a born communicator with an easy laugh. My adoptive father communicated with an adding machine, not phrases. He taught me honesty and hard work—but I never had his desires to play golf or figure taxes. Who was I really born to be? Wasn't there more than just being raised?

I would never know.

Then, one cold winter afternoon I received an email with a scientific offer I couldn't resist. When I saw how DNA testing, "genetic genealogy," could reveal a biological family tree, the desire to know this hidden half of my family, the first seeds of my existence, came blazing back to life with an energy that surprised me. Although I protested weakly for a while, I soon found myself consumed with a search that would rapidly obsess me and change everything I knew about family.

1

TIME TO SPIT OR GET OFF THE POT

My adoptive mother, Pat, often says, "Life can change with a phone call." She's right. She's been on this Earth since 1934, long enough to attest to the fragility of life. "Attitude is everything," she says. Her experience is rich, but her technology skills are poor. She's not on a computer and still has a flip-phone waiting for a voicemail box to be set up. But our worlds aren't really that far apart. Pat's phone call, my email—it makes no difference how the news is delivered. One little unexpected message can change everything. And for me, that email came in December 2013.

Christmas stinks for "news gatherers." Not Christmas itself, but that whole, lost chunk of time between Thanksgiving and New Year's. Nothing new ever goes on—the last big thing that happened for me during that period involved college finals. I loathe how the whole world agrees to "just wait until after the holidays." That's the way it is every December, and while many people enjoy having time to celebrate, it doesn't bode well for my business.

You can't make up news. It either happens or it doesn't. On the upside, as the weatherman on Houston's KPRC 2, I get plenty of extra air-time. People need to know the travel and shopping weather! I show pictures of my viewers' amazing holiday lights, and I love the photos of the screaming kids whose parents have forced them on the mall-Santa's lap. Our newsroom email boxes fill up with dozens of PR releases, usually light-hearted story ideas that make these days of good-will-toward-men even more special than they already are. If we can't find a happy story, then the public relations world can always be relied upon.

So in 2013, it didn't surprise me when my news co-anchor, Dominique Sachse, forwarded me a feel-good email from Donna, a PR specialist.

Take a look at this, you might be interested! read the subject line.

I've worked with Dominique since 1995, and she's like a sister to me. Beautiful inside and out, she has my best interests at heart. I count myself lucky that Dominique and Bill Balleza, our television co-anchor, are such good friends. For years, we have hosted "anchor dinners" at each other's homes with our spouses. We've watched each other's children grow up, shared our take on the TV world, celebrated life's joys and consoled each other in the sad times. When viewers sense our chemistry on air, it's because we really are a TV family.

So if Dominique thought I'd be interested, I figured I would be. I clicked through to the link. Every Christmas she gives me an amazingly great tie which she proudly admits comes from the cheapest place she can find. It's her mission. But for Christmas 2013 she sent me much more than a tie, and it came with a whole lot more knots.

The press release headline jumped out at me.

Adopted man, Brian Mixom, reunites with long lost family thanks to the science of DNA, just in time for the Christmas holiday!

The "adopted" part caught my attention. Dominique, Bill, and practically everyone else who knows me, know I'm adopted. It's such a comfortable part of who I am. When we've aired adoption stories over the years, I explain to the viewing audience that I, too, am an adoptee. I encourage adoption. Each year I emcee the luncheon held by Arms Wide Open Adoption Services, a group dedicated to building families through adoption.

Yet, at first read, this happy story of an adopted man finding his family didn't seem to have much to do with me. Good for him, I thought. I appreciated Dominique thinking of me, but really didn't pay much attention to it. So Brian found his "real" parents—a term that has always made me shudder a bit. We all know that *real* parents are not necessarily the ones who make you, but the ones who "make" you. That could be a grandmother, a big brother, a school coach, or anyone brave enough to step up. The ones who wipe your butt and wipe your tears—they are your family, earning that title in every sense of the word. And in my case, Pat and Jimmy took over the task and they, along with my sister, Sharon, became my nuclear family with no regrets. As Jimmy's work as a CPA for oil companies moved us from Arkansas to Mississippi and eventually to Birmingham, Alabama, we were a real family.

That evening after dinner, I was lying on the love seat in the kitchen, going through emails. Kevin and I built our house in 1997, and while it is not the fanciest home in Houston, it's perfect for us—the outside painted a true butter yellow, inside painted in soft colors with names like Autumn Rain, and filled with comfortable furniture. The heart of our home is the kitchen. We moved our breakfast table out of the kitchen long ago, seeing that it was only used twice a year when my parents visited and sat there to eat Rice Krispies. We replaced it with this big, cream-colored, corduroy love seat. It's my go-to every morning with my coffee, a computer, a TV, and River and Ocean, our schnauzers, one black, one white. Now, lounging in this very safe place, I was going through the day's emails, when I saw Dominique's again. Away from the busy noise of the newsroom, I read it again more carefully.

"Take a look at this," I said to Kevin. "It's amazing what they can do with DNA now."

"Wow," he said after he read it. "Maybe if you did this, you could do a feature on the newscast." Using the science of DNA intrigued me. I didn't know much about how DNA worked, but anything science is interesting to me.

"Maybe," I said. "It could make a good story." We talked about it, and neither of us thought there'd be much more in it than that—a chance to locate a distant cousin somewhere.

That night, I found myself lying awake wrestling with the thought of doing a search and admitting to myself that I'd always wondered exactly how I got into this world. Am I a product of a spring romance or a Spring Break dance? Just who were those folks who had me, but couldn't keep me? Or just didn't want to keep me? Shouldnt't I get in touch to at least thank them for giving me a better life?

And, like anyone, I always feared there might be health issues lurking in my family tree as well. Sadly, I'd watched Alzheimer's, ALS, cancer, and heart disease ravage members of my extended adopted family. But no matter how much I had wondered about such things, the fact that Arkansas was a closed-records state daunted any serious search I might have made to find answers. On top of that, I had learned in a random conversation on a plane that the hospital where I was born had burned down in the 1960s. At that point, I figured that any chance to find my biological family had gone up in smoke.

Now, Dominique's email had me revisiting a subject that I thought was closed forever. Did I want to dive into a DNA search? Digging for information is definitely part of my genetic makeup, and unraveling the mystery was intriguing to me, as was the opportunity to learn about the science. The answer was easy from that point of view: of course! And Kevin was right; I could make a great two-minute feature piece out of the process and whatever I discovered.

Then I started thinking about my sister Sharon's search for her biological parents, and the answer didn't seem as easy.

Two years after I was born in Arkansas and adopted by Pat and Jimmy, Sharon was born in a private unwed mother's home in Jacksonville, Florida. From the time she was a little girl, she wanted to know about her family of origin. A sense of abandonment always haunted her, and she felt if she only knew where she came from, she wouldn't feel so empty.

Growing up together, she would tell me she felt alone in the world. I knew Pat and Jimmy loved her immensely and we had a large community of friends. But Sharon seemed to have a different experience than the rest of us. Where Pat and I were extroverted, always at the center of the action, and Jimmy was absorbed in his work and his golf, Sharon didn't seem as comfortable. People filled my life through baseball, student government, my high school fraternity, church group, and all sorts of clubs. Sharon was athletic, too, but she was drawn to swimming, an individual sport. Pat encouraged her to participate in all the Southern social rituals, but she wasn't interested.

I was too busy working on being the best-all-round boy to really notice. Being gay at that time and in that place, I was making up for any difference I was beginning to feel, and somehow thinking I had to make up for being adopted, to make Pat and Jimmy glad that they had chosen me. No Give-Backs! I was a kid, though, so I didn't really

My sister Sharon and I, we had a very happy childhood.

get any of this at the time. I just knew Sharon felt sad, and she thought finding out about her birth parents would make her feel better.

Fortunately for her, when the time came, the task of a parental search turned out to be easy. She simply wrote a letter to the unwed mother's home in 1995 and asked to connect with her biological family. Florida is a sealed-records state, but that didn't mean the private home was, so, her family search worked like a dating app today: "I want to meet you, if you want to meet me." Swipe Right! The home wrote her family on record and, *bam!* It could not have been more simple or, as it turned out, more sad.

She phoned me as soon as she got the results. "My mother's dead," she said. I could hear an exasperated pain in her voice.

"What? You're kidding? What happened?" *Good Lord*, I thought. The woman she's been wondering about all her life. Dead. Great.

"She had uterine cancer and died in 1977," Sharon said, beginning to cry. "Her husband isn't my father, and he never knew about me, but the home convinced him who I am. He told me she was in and out of hospitals for five years before she died."

"I'm so sorry," I said. Knowing how devastating this news must be to her after so many years of hope for a happy ending, I couldn't think of anything to say that might be comforting.

She pulled herself together and went on. "I have half brothers and a half sister, who basically had to raise themselves because she was so sick."

It had turned out that her half sister, Lauren, taught elementary art and, coincidentally, lived fairly close to me in Houston

"Can you have dinner with her?" Sharon asked.

"Of course," I told Sharon. When I met Lauren at Macaroni Grill a few weeks later, I could see she shared flawless skin with Sharon, a blessing that has always made me a little jealous. To deal with the skin I inherited, I had crammed down Tetracycline as a kid with a glass of milk every morning, only to find out years later that milk pretty much voids its effect.

After we visited, Lauren spearheaded a reunion for herself and her brothers—Carl in Georgia and Joey in Indiana—to meet Sharon. So in October 1996 they all converged at my house with stories of their childhood and adulthood, pictures of their shared mother, hugs and laughs, but admittedly a forced comfort. Not so much a reunion of shared memories, more of a sip-and-see with strangers.

Sharon learned that her bio-mother's cancer battle had been a long and arduous journey, often from a hospital bed. The kids learned their way around a package of hot dogs and a boiling pot of water at a very young age. Practically raising themselves, their world was not the homemade-dinner-on-the-table world Sharon had experienced, and she realized for the first time just how easy she'd had it. And while her biological mother had died, her biological father might as well have.

"His name is Bob Bailey," she said. "Isn't there a song about him?" She tried to laugh.

"You're thinking of Tom Dooley," I said, "the Confederate soldier who murdered his girlfriend." I remembered that old song and at the same time wondered, "What now?" Sharon had never gotten many breaks.

"Well, he's not a murderer. He's alive and never knew about me. He was a sailor in Jacksonville, passing through. So he sent me his picture and a note and said that he has a family now and doesn't want anything to do with me." She sighed. "He doesn't want to interrupt his family life with me suddenly. So that's all I get. One picture."

Sharon handled the news admirably—I couldn't imagine spending my whole life creating an idea of who my biological parents were, struggling with abandonment issues, wrestling with the emotions of making a family search and anticipating a reunion with the person who fathered me, only to get one Kodak still-shot and a brush off. It seemed cowardly and cruel. All I could think was, "Hang down *your* head, Bob Bailey."

Although the whole experience brought Sharon the closure she sought—for better or worse—it seemed to me that she had gone through a lot of emotional pain just to get an occasional holiday update from a long-lost half sister. Sharon, however, saw it differently: "I had to know, and now I know."

Now, unable to sleep in the quiet house, I wondered, "Do I have to know, too?"

Sharon and I had both been in our thirties when she went looking for her birth family, and her experience solidified for me why I didn't want to search for my *real* parents. Hers had turned out to be a little too real—one real dead and the other real mean. So thinking about her experience gave me pause. Aside from the emotional end-play, my adoption in Arkansas made a birth search very difficult, if not impossible. How would I go about that, anyway? Private investigators? Lawyers? Watergate burglars? I had no idea. I envisioned sitting in the Library of Congress with a Starbucks latte, thumbing through pages and pages of birth records and certificates trying to find a secret number. And to what end?

Would finding out I might get some crippling disease do me any good? I remember reading that Arlo Guthrie's father, Woody, died of Huntington's disease, and Arlo was offered a test to find out if he might develop it. He refused. He simply didn't want to know: It's not worth thinking about! Arlo's reasoning is pretty simple—none of us will get out of here alive.

Would I ignite new relationships? Did anyone really hold a torch for me in the fourth quarter of his or her life? Why upset other people's apple carts for a yearly Christmas card? Who goes there?

Brian Mixom did. According to the press release, he had been reunited with his family just in time to exchange holiday gifts. His biological mother had been living only two miles away from him, and he never knew it. When he finally tracked her down, she had just died. He had missed her by *that* much! There she had been all these years, on the other side of the cul-de-sac, maybe swerving to avoid her own biological son playing catch in the middle of the street, so close to reuniting with this child she gave up. The upcoming Christmas feast would have his newly discovered half siblings sitting at the table, but no mom and no dad. And here's Brian, now 58 years old, advising earnestly and cheerfully: "If my story can inspire people to make these connections earlier, then I am happy to tell it."

The story went on to describe the Family Tree DNA lab where they tested Brian's DNA. It happened to be located right here in Houston. Any doubts I had about what I might find if I took the DNA plunge were overshadowed by the fact that it all seemed like a parlor game to me.

Somehow, *this amazing new science* led Brian to other people who shared enough DNA with him to determine a relationship. That's about all I understood at the time: *If I match some of your DNA and you match some of mine, then we are related.* The next step would be measuring how much DNA I actually share with anyone else—and that will tell us how closely we are related. Simple.

And I couldn't ignore a significant part of Brian Mixom's story, which rang a bit like my sister's: Brian's bio-mother had been alive *only a year earlier* living two miles away from him. I recalled my dermatologist's story of his adopted brother finding his birth mother, who turned out to be a nurse one hospital over.

Brian Mixom and I are only five years apart in age. Whenever I had asked Pat about my biological parents, she told me that they were both 18 years old at my birth, unmarried, and simply in no financial position to take care of me. My biological mother was pretty and smart, while bio-dad had great athletic ability.

"Mom, what would I be like if I were your real son?" I would ask.

"Not as good," Pat always answered. "Not as good."

That's all my mother said she knew, so that's all I ever knew. Brian's story inspired me. With DNA, there was so much more to know. I might be able to find these athletic, handsome bio-parents of mine. But there might not be enough time, if I didn't hurry. What if my biological mother or father lived down the road? What if they even watched me on television for the latest forecast? For the first time in my life, I really felt like I needed to find some answers.

I have always joked that my mother found me in a woven basket floating in the bulrushes of the Arkansas River, somewhat like Moses, perhaps the long lost lovechild of Marilyn Monroe and John F. Kennedy. I mean, if JFK and Marilyn ever *did* have a love child, what better place to stash him than Little Rock, Arkansas? Not even J. Edgar Hoover would find me there. Perhaps the time had finally arrived to take the plunge from the woven basket of my imagination into the river of my DNA-reality.

I finally fell asleep that night telling myself that Kevin was right: everyone knew I was adopted, and, no matter what I discovered, a story on the newscast on this intriguing genetic genealogy was a great idea.

My TV weather office, like most, sits quietly in the studio away from the newsroom, bustling only as the newscast approaches. If there was any noise that next afternoon, I don't remember it, as I reflected over the press release and picked up the phone to call Kevin.

"What do you think?" I asked. "Should I do this?" I had felt so sure the night before, but now I felt nervous about finding out too much. And especially nervous about making Pat and Jimmy feel like they weren't enough. I certainly didn't want to imply I had a need for new parents. But there was a mystery here, and like every good detective from Encyclopedia Brown to Sherlock Holmes, I was determined to find the clues and see where they led.

Kevin listened to me elaborate about all the pros and cons. Then, in his usual pragmatic way, he cut through my emotional interpretation and gave me an objective viewpoint.

"Yes," he said emphatically. "Your sister found out a lot about her medical history and that made all the difference. In fact, it probably saved her life." I hadn't even thought of that. Sharon's mother's death from uterine cancer got her off the fence to have a hysterectomy. He went on. "I'm actually kind of surprised you've never looked before." Kevin is the caretaker in the family, the one who's at Walgreens for me when I have the slightest sniffle. He flosses every day. Not to mention his face product regimen. I should have anticipated his reaction would be from a human resources approach, which is exactly what he does for a living.

"There you go," I thought. Medical history seemed reason enough. After all, I'd spent decades filling out in-patient forms asking about family diseases by simply writing "adopted" at the top of the page.

Full of determination, I hung up, ready to get to work on this important story. The studio came back into focus. I looked over my shoulder, as if the cameras all around the room were watching me. Holding my breath a little, I wrote Public Relations Specialist Donna an email:

> *Dominique passed your press release regarding Brian Mixom to me and I'd like to pursue this for personal reasons. I am also adopted (from a Little Rock hospital) and would be interested in Family Tree DNA. Can you provide me some info on how to submit my DNA and who to talk to?*

I finally hit "send" in between my afternoon weathercasts and went to drawing a low-temperature map.

My email dinged back almost immediately:

> *I can help!*

2

IT'S A BIG DEAL

I wasn't expecting to hear back from Donna so quickly, but I was delighted. Her response told me exactly what to expect from DNA testing:

Here's how it works in a nutshell: The kit arrives by mail and gives step-by-step instructions on how to supply your sample. Inside the kit is a plastic vial (a.k.a. the Collection Kit). You then swab your mouth, as the directions indicate. Once this process and paperwork are complete, you send it off in the addressed envelope. Then the company contacts you via email with the results in anywhere from four to six weeks. Please be on the lookout from Morgan Hawthorne with Family Tree DNA. Morgan will answer your questions and step you through the entire process. Good luck and I can't wait to see what you find out!

Being a good detective, or borderline stalker, depending on how you define my tendency to research everyone I meet, I Facebooked Morgan and took a second glance at the "Victoria's Secret Model picture from her former life." Morgan serves as Family Tree DNA's Data Assurance Analyst, and even on Facebook, it was clear that she's a very smart woman, balancing work and life with a sense of humor. I saw where she'd been given credit for her work on an episode of "Finding Your Roots." A wife and mother, her dark hair and perfect smile make her a shoe-in for Victoria's Secret.

"Oh, Lord," she laughed when I mentioned it in our first phone call. "That whole thing was just a joke, but thanks!"

We set up lunch at the Houstonian to go over the different tests offered by her company. Over a southwestern Caesar salad, the young woman who would become my very patient mentor in my scientific journey began to fill me in on the process.

"As an adoptee, you really should get everything analyzed," she said between bites. "We need to run all the DNA tests available for as much information as we can get about you."

"More than one?" I asked, thinking, "How much DNA does one person have, for Pete's sake?"

"It's actually the same cheek swab, just analyzed for different types of DNA," said Morgan. "Let's start by talking about Y-DNA, which is probably the easiest to understand."

If there is one DNA lesson I learned in ninth-grade biology, it's that we have 23 pairs of chromosomes. On that magical 23rd chromosome we either have two X chromosomes or one X and one Y. If you have XX you are a girl, made of sugar and spice, and if you have XY you are snips and snails and puppy dog tails. How a person ends up identifying within their gender is a completely different story, as are genetic mutations.

Mothers can only give their child an X, since they are XX. Clearly, they have no Y to pass down. Dad can pass on his X or his Y, and that's what happens. A daughter gets one X from Mom and Dad's one X. A son gets one X from Mom and Dad's one Y. The fathers will *always* pass the X down to his daughters and will *always* pass the Y down to his sons. It can't work any other way. In fact, the Y goes directly from father to son, generation to generation, which is a "key to the tree."

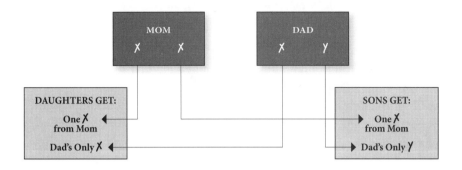

Morgan recommended I get the Y-DNA test done. After all, my Y-DNA came straight from whoever turned out to be my biological father, just as his came from his father, and his from his father, and so on. That Y-DNA has been passed right down the daddy line from father to son forever.

"But how does that help me? I don't know who my biological father is," I asked. "Obviously, I got a Y from my dad, but it's not like some guy's name was stamped on it. Right?"

"Here's the easy part for males, because males get the Y," Morgan explained. "Let's suppose a man two hundred years ago named John Smith started having sons who had sons and had sons. What would their last name be?"

"Smith," I said, feeling like I'd scored.

"Exactly. And their Y-DNA ultimately goes back to that John Smith who is a great-great-great-grandfather to all of them. So if you share the Y with a lot of other men who have also tested their Y-DNA, then the same or similar last name will show up. In this case, you'd share Y-DNA with a lot of Smiths. So that is most likely the last name of your biological father, meaning your last name, too!"

That's when I had the first of many "duh" moments: this whole DNA discovery will only work if a whole lot of other people have joined in. And those participating will somehow have to be related to me. An adoption search, no matter what the scientific breakthroughs we've made, is still about finding a name.

"Secondly," Morgan continued, "On the off chance that your biological father or any brothers have tested *their* Y-DNA, then we might find a really strong Y-match with yours and theirs—after all, you'd all share the same Y-DNA. That is probably too much to hope for, but you never know."

Morgan finished her salad, let the waiter clear the table and pulled out a regular deck of playing cards.

"Texas hold 'em?" I asked, smiling.

"Ha! No, a little DNA lesson," she said. "You understand cards, right?" She looked at me as if she occasionally got a negative on that one. I nodded, sparing her the history of my card-playing expertise, and she went on. "Let's make this simple. Here's your mom and all her DNA." She handed me all the red cards—diamonds and hearts.

♥ 2 3 4 5 6 7 8 9 10 J Q K A ♦ 2 3 4 5 6 7 8 9 10 J Q K A

"Dad's DNA is all the black cards," she said, and spread them on the table.

♣ 2 3 4 5 6 7 8 9 10 J Q K A ♠ 2 3 4 5 6 7 8 9 10 J Q K A

Okay, the DNA deck is divided, red cards and black cards, I thought. Easy enough.

"So," she continued, "when they created you, you got half your DNA from Mom's pile and half from Dad's pile." She shuffled the 26 red cards and dealt 13 to a pile. Then she did the same with the black cards and pointed. "That's you—that's your DNA."

Morgan continued. "So when creating you, your mom and dad gave you half of their 26 cards…you would get exactly 13 *randomly* dealt cards from each of them. That's where your DNA comes from. Take a look." In a genetic sense, we really do have to play the hand we're dealt.

I looked at my playing cards of DNA and saw a nice mix:

♣ 5 6 9 Q K ♠ 2 3 4 5 8 9 J K
♥ 2 3 4 5 8 10 J Q ♦ 3 9 J Q A

"Now, give me the cards back," she instructed. "We need to make you a brother and then sister." Morgan went through the whole procedure two more times.

Brother: ♥ 3 4 6 8 Q K   ♦ 2 3 6 7 10 J Q K   ♣ 2 8 9 10 Q   ♠ 2 5 7 8 9 Q A

Sister: ♥ 2 3 5 10 J Q   ♦ 2 3 5 9 10 J K   ♣ 5 6 8 9 J Q   ♠ 2 6 7 8 9 J K

Me: ♥ 2 3 4 5 8 10 J Q   ♦ 3 9 J Q A   ♣ 5 6 9 Q K   ♠ 2 3 4 5 8 9 J K

Literally, this "big deal" analogy really brought it home. Comparing the cards, I could see how I shared different, specific cards with my imaginary brother and other cards with my imaginary sister. And we all shared 10 between the three of us. So we could be counted on to share a lot of traits, but certainly we would be different—just like real siblings. Full-siblings share about half of their DNA and half-siblings share about 25% of their DNA.

"The point is, you share enough cards between the three of you that we can determine you are all from the same parents, and therefore that you are all siblings," Morgan explained.

Of course, in the real world of DNA, we're not counting just 26 cards from a playing deck. In order to determine relationships, you have to count 750,000 pieces of DNA from the full 3 billion pieces in the genome—*that* is what actually happens—and why it takes a few weeks to test DNA, if you want it done right. Quality assurance.

"So that's the simple version of how DNA works," Morgan told me. "The source, or deck of cards, may be the same, but the deal is different from person to person, which is what makes us all different!"

"That explains why there are always the brothers who look nothing alike," I said, nodding.

In a real sense, the chips fall where they may, and the cards get dealt. DNA gets reshuffled and re-dealt from generation to generation. So while Grandma might have passed a two of clubs to your mother, and Mom might have passed that same two of clubs to your sister, you might not get it. After all, over many generations the decks become more and more shuffled; so much so that a distant cousin may not share even enough DNA to measure, while his brother could share 1% or more. All kinds of combinations can happen as DNA gets spread out over the decades. Especially with those first American families: they all arrived here pretty much in the first two hundred years, and their DNA did a lot of mingling, producing what Morgan explained is called "Colonial Soup."

So, once my DNA was tested, I would be looking at as many other people's tests as I could find and matching my cards to theirs—the stronger the matches, the closer the relatives.

Here's a rough chart as to a relationship based on percentage of DNA:

100% = you're identical twins

50% = you're the parent or the child

50% = you're siblings

25% = you're half siblings

25% = this is what you share with grandparents/aunts/uncles

12% = first cousins/great-uncles/great-aunts/great-grandparents

6% = a first cousin once removed

3% = second cousins

.5 to 1% = third cousins

Less than half a percent = distant cousins (4th, 5th, 6th)

"Can't they get more precise?" I asked Morgan.

"No," she said. "A rough chart is as good as it gets, because there is that chance you might share a lot of cards with one person and not another, even if they share a lot between them. It's just how DNA works when it recombines, and it's why top scientists will tell you that good old-fashioned genealogy and documentation can often be the best way to find family. DNA is often only the proof to something you already suspect."

I had no documentation or genealogy, so I realized that once my test results came back, I would have to go with the hope that rough chart offered.

Morgan was very generous with her time that afternoon, as she would be in the future. I had many questions for her, and the combination of hard science and good old-fashioned sleuthing had me hooked. I was ready to sign on the dotted line and spit wherever they told me.

By the end of lunch, I had learned that these different DNA tests promised to reveal the following:

- Y-DNA would (maybe) give me my biological father's last name and would find some distant male cousins, maybe even a brother, with the same last name.
- Autosomal DNA, called Family Finder, would find lots of relatives, from Viking cousins who shared just a little bit of DNA (less than 0.5%), to first cousins (12%), to a long lost brother (25% if half, 50% if full), or even a parent (50%)! I would also get an ethnic breakdown.

Like any card game, you don't win if you don't play—and, in this case, I wouldn't win unless a lot of other people played. If everyone in the world tested his or her DNA, we'd know how to put together the world's family tree. But, of course, not everyone does—and there are plenty of good reasons why, many of which I'd experienced myself.

As we wrapped up our lunch, I expressed how enthusiastic I was about getting started. Morgan looked steadily across the table at me.

"Let me leave you with a word of caution," she said. "Another reason people don't look too closely at their DNA is outright fear: you may find out you are really a Johnson instead of a Smith. And wasn't Grandma Brown's neighbor named Johnson?" She gave me a knowing look. "That can get awkward."

"Well, let's order all the tests you have." I laughed, brushing off any concerns. "I can handle awkward." After all, I had already been through the most awkward moment of my life twenty-five years before—the kind of awkward moment that has torn many families apart.

3

MY WALK-IN CLOSET

"We have to talk," she said in her deep Bea Arthur voice, laced with Southern country club. I love my mother's voice. It's as comfortable to my ear as warm biscuits are to the morning, perfect for soothing a scraped knee or a bruised ego. This is the voice that, over and over, read me the Bible and *The Chosen Child*, our go-to thin, gray book explaining my adoption, "all your aunts and uncles threw a big party for you and brought you gifts, they were so happy you were part of the family."

When I got the call, I was working in Biloxi and had come home between the evening and late newscasts. I had just popped a Stouffer's spinach soufflé in the oven when the phone rang—the regular phone, the kind we all had in 1987.

It was my mom, Pat. "Mrs. B" my friends all called her. Pat had grown up with pricey cars and upstairs maids. She generally viewed life through rose-colored glasses, but I could tell from her tone that those shades had turned dark right now. She's been known to go after snakes with sticks. And I knew that we had to talk. I had known it for a long time.

"Sure." I tried to be nonchalant, but it didn't work.

"You are 27 years old, Frank, and I haven't heard a thing about a girl in four years."

"Well, Mom, you don't hear everything about—"

"Are you gay?" she asked before I could finish. She planted the stick right on the snake's neck. Pat never buries the lead.

Pat and I have always been tight. Sharing the same June 22nd birthday bonds us, we both have easy smiles and we like to laugh. We've always been honest with each other.

I took a deep breath. "Well, I'm not going to lie to you." I couldn't, and I wouldn't. She had the guts to ask; I had to find the guts to answer. I had thought about this conversation many times, but in my mind it never occurred this abruptly.

Just as I was about to speak, she shouted to my father, who was clearly in another part of the house, likely with his nose in the newspaper.

"Ji-i-i-m-m-m-y-y-y! Pi-i-i-ck u-u-u-p! I *told* you! He i-i-i-is!"

I shuddered, imagining the debate they'd had the hour before, arguing over whether I was or wasn't and whether to call me and confront this situation or just let it go and allow the truth to settle into our lives by osmosis, simply smiling and dancing around the pink elephant in the room. So very Deep South.

My dad picked up the extension. "This doesn't seem normal to me," he said, without a greeting beforehand. "But if it does to you, then it must be. I know you're not stupid." He's always the pragmatic one in our group, with advice about avoiding debt, staying away from fights, and choosing wisely. He's a solid Presbyterian, which means life is what it is, and there's not much you can do about it. He continued, "You wouldn't do something to hurt yourself, so this must be who you are."

My father doesn't stew. He stated his thoughts, and moved on. My mother, however, invented stewing. And, to add to her pain in that moment, she had lost her father the year before. I knew she felt like she would lose me now to some strange, dangerous community. The spinach soufflé burnt to a crisp that night, and, over the next two weeks, we talked as a family for many hours.

I finally convinced my very traditional parents, in some delicate way, that no one's life would change—not much—and that if they really wanted the back story, then there were plenty of professionals to talk to and books to read, even friends and family they already knew who were gay. Built-in comfort and consultation. I gently suggested they try some lavender spectacles, for once.

Their concern centered on me, of course, and my career and my happiness. They love me, and never—before or after that conversation—have they sought to bring about fear or shame over any aspect of my life. But they were also experienced, and they knew the rest of the world might not be so sympathetic.

With my parents, Pat and Jimmy, in the mid 90s.

Mom took the Southerner's pragmatic approach: "Don't talk about it." Dad continued to hold to his initial thought: he trusted that I wasn't stupid, I knew who I was and I should be careful. That was that.

My first foray out of the closet to open up to my parents ranked high as an awkward family moment, but our family emerged from it with a new understanding. Although Pat and Jimmy had very different reactions, as I would have expected, they both showed their character and their love for me. Once we had communicated and cleared the air, I realized that there had been no need for me to put off that conversation as long as I had.

I should have guessed how my dad would react. He had raised Sharon and me to treat people right, follow our conscience, and go to Sunday school and church every single week. He worked hard to give us the best education possible, so we would be strong and independent. I can think of no better example of his approach than when he informed me that after graduation the Daddy Dollars would come to an abrupt end.

"I'm looking forward to your graduation," he had announced in 1981 when I was home from Washington & Lee University for Christmas break my senior year.

"Thanks," I said. I thought this sounded a bit foreboding. "Why?"

"I can stop paying your car insurance."

"That would be weird," I thought. I didn't have a clue how much it even cost. "Uh, then who's going to pay it?"

He pointed right at me. "You are. Along with the rest of your bills." After all, I would be 21. At the time, his salt-of-the-earth personality felt a lot more salty than earthy, but the nest nudge turned out to be the smartest, and best, thing he could have done for me.

These two people with luck in their own life had adopted me, and I think it just rubbed off on me. Or, I sometimes think they taught me how to turn opportunity into luck. Whichever it was, luck or opportunity, I found a job as a TV weatherman: I had interned my senior year in college at a TV station in Roanoke, Virginia, training to be a reporter. Instead of a news job, in what was probably a desperate moment, they offered me a weekend weather job.

"*Weather*? I don't even know all 50 states!" I protested honestly. Of course I knew we had 50, but I had no idea where they all were. The South I had figured out, but the West with all those big squares puzzled me, not to mention all the little pieces of the Northeast. But my bosses had seen enough personality to take a chance on me. And, adding hard work to the luck of that opportunity, I've found being a meteorologist to be as reward-ing a career as any I could have imagined. And I learned my states.

Now that I was determined to do this DNA thing, as Pat and Jimmy's son and with my experience, I had to believe that luck and opportunity would carry me to the answers I sought. But when Morgan left me with that mysterious warning about what I might uncover along the way, I began to think hard about how any "new" relatives might react to my being gay. And I still had an underlying concern that embarking on a search with so much potential to find answers might somehow hurt my aging parents' feelings.

After enthusiastic, let's-do-this-goodbyes to Morgan, I sat in the car for a minute before I turned it on, thinking about family, and specifically about Jimmy. I remembered that after my sister's experience, my father must have realized a closed-adoption would take a lot more effort than Sharon's had. The year she got married and started building her family,

My dad and I on my first Easter, 1961.

I could tell he and Pat were a little worried about me being alone. Out of the blue one day he offered: "I'll foot the bill if you want to try and find them."

"No thanks," I said, only half-joking. "I've come out of the closet to one family and I'm not coming out to another." He gave me a half smile.

At the time, I thought that these conversations and the progress I had made with my traditional, conservative family was all the coming out I really needed to do. I had no idea how quickly my reality would change, or how it would make me more thankful than ever that Pat and Jimmy were the ones who made me their chosen child.

4

AISLE BE THERE

"Stan Smith, Hartford Insurance." A nice-looking forty-something, slightly balding guy in a gray suit and a loose tie stuck out his hand.

I laughed as I shook it. "Frank Billingsley, Gay Groom."

He smiled, looked around, and then laughed himself. "I think I'm at the wrong party."

"Yep, your party is two floors down," I pointed downward, "but at least now you have a great story for everyone, right?" I grinned. He agreed and I can only imagine how far that wrong-party story carried him.

That day, I would have greeted anyone I met with a laugh and a smile and a hearty welcome. It was a day that I had often thought would never come. Once my parents determined that I was indeed gay, they had been concerned about how I would connect with the world. And although I had a great deal more perspective on the situation than they did, finding a partner is a challenge that consumes most of us, no matter where we identify on the gender spectrum—until we find the right person.

Whether we are adopted or biological, half or whole, found or not found—no matter our family of origin—above all there is the family we create. People joke that you can pick your friends but not your family. Plenty of friends become family, and we can choose the person we fall in love with, throw all our trust into, and stand beside through thick-and-thin. We bring in children or dogs or cats or goldfish or all of it, and then we build a home. The family recipe has a lot of ingredients.

Despite any concerns my family or I might have had along the way about me creating a new branch of our tree, I had finally met the man of

Our young family at a Kevin's sister's wedding in 1996.

my dreams. If Stan the Insurance Man had wanted to stay and dance at our wedding, I would have been happy to include him. It was a day for celebration. But his insurance party called, so Stan offered his congratulations and got back on the elevator.

I had met Kevin on August 12, 1995, while actually on a date at a local honky-tonk with a guy who'd been giving me the runaround (compatibility issues), and Kevin struggled in the middle of his divorce (also compatibility issues). As Kevin's personal life had changed, and his seven-year marriage ended, my professional life was also changing. Earlier in the year, I had taken on the responsibility as chief meteorologist at KPRC. I felt professionally complete but longed to find that personal commitment. I was 35, and Kevin was 28.

Kevin had met his wife in high school, and they dated right into their college years. Although they took precautions, even the best methods can fail, and she got pregnant. They found themselves with a baby on the way when they were 20 years old—technically still minors themselves. They were already engaged, however, so the date just got moved up a bit. Truly excited, Kevin couldn't wait to marry and become a father, but I must say—and it's become a bit of a joke now—in his wedding album he is the *only one* smiling. Not his parents. Not her parents. Not his sister. Not her sister. Not her. Nobody else smiled.

But marry they did, coincidentally on my parent's wedding date, November 28th. In March 1988, a bouncing, beautiful baby boy arrived. They named him Morgan. Like any young family, they struggled with finances, education, and parenting. You can only hit so many curve balls until you finally, simply, strike out. They filed for divorce in early 1995 and, lucky for me, that August, a friend of Kevin's insisted he go out for a night on the town to get his mind off everything.

So when we met, I had that not-so-great date going, but I connected with Kevin and got his last name. Of course, I got the name wrong. I called directory assistance—we're still in the twentieth century here, remember—the next day.

"I think it's Gilliland. Or Gilland, or Gillard?" I said, giving her a little background on why I wasn't exactly sure.

She just laughed. "Hmmm, no, let me see—" She put me on hold for what seemed an eternity. "I have a Kevin *Gilliard*! Try that!" Then in her sweet, Southern voice, she added, "And good luck, honey!"

I should mention that Kevin has always looked younger than he is. Even today, close to 50, he could pass for 35. When I met him, he looked 22. As the phone rang, I felt a few flutters.

"Hello?"

I knew he looked young, but I hadn't remembered his voice being so high. "Uh, um," I stuttered. "Um, Kevin?"

"Hold on," he replied. "Da-a-ad!"

I almost fell off my chair. *Dad?* And this child is old enough to answer the phone? I was about to hang up when Kevin came on the line. He explained—simply stated, really—that he had a seven-year-old son.

"So, um, should we *all* go to dinner tonight?" I asked, not sure on protocol but trying to be gallant. But Kevin smartly didn't want to introduce Morgan to me until he really felt the relationship might stick. He didn't want a slew of "uncles" coming into his child's life.

We discovered quickly that this relationship would take, and I met Morgan a week later. By early 1996, we were living together, creating our family. I won't pretend that things are always perfect, but we came into the relationship as adults, and that helps. Our arguments were mostly about parenting, in fact. Given that all of us in life were brought up just a little bit differently, it's no surprise that we bring slightly different parenting techniques to the table. And we generally think of our own as the best, of course. That can give rise to a few disagreements!

What has helped our relationship survive 20 years is, fortunately, coming from the "same place." Both of our sets of parents are still together and are strong in their faith (his Catholic and mine Presbyterian). We each have one sibling, and we have similar educations. I do believe that opposites certainly attract, but so does sameness. A person's background is their foundation for the future. If you're lucky enough to fall in love with someone who shares a similar foundation, it helps you to forge a strong life together.

Two years into our relationship we decided to buy a vacant lot with nothing but a water oak on the corner and build our own house from scratch: *that* will break you or make you as a couple in a matter of weeks. My weather career had proven to me that if you set your mind to something, even if you know very little about it, you can succeed. So we plunged into the world of builders and blueprints and decisions.

Just a bathroom alone can drive you insane: Chrome fixtures? Brass? Nickel? Chrome and brass? Square, round, oval, rectangle? Granite, marble, slabs, tiles? If you've ever been to a plumbing aisle and stared at the wall of showerhead options and become overwhelmed, then you have a small inkling of what it's like to build a house. Multiply that feeling by a million, and then factor in having to make all of those building decisions with your significant other, knowing that even if *you've* decided on something it may very well not be the final word.

Many times we wondered why we didn't just buy a pretty little condo already up and running! But nothing good ever comes easy, they say, and we got through it. We've lived happily in our butter yellow, kind-of-Mediterranean-style house since 1997, and I'm sure we're stronger and smarter for the experience.

Kevin is an HR specialist. Colleges didn't even offer a human resources degree when he attended—remember when they called it "personnel?" Consequently, he has worked his way up in an international I.T. solutions company, and he does HR very well. The benefit for me is that he's really good at seeing all sides of any argument! The downside is he usually wins.

If I've learned any guidelines for a successful relationship, they are pretty simple: never make your partner feel jealous or worried, and always make your partner look good. If you treat your partner as well as you treat your boss, then you'll get along just fine.

So we have charged forward together, Kevin and I, for the past two decades. In 2011 we announced to our friends at our annual Christmas Eve party that we were engaged to be married. Some states had already passed marriage equality, but when New York did so in July of that year, we were over-the-moon excited and decided that we would take the plunge in the Empire State. I like to think we put the "man" in Manhattan. We would both have preferred to marry in Houston, but that option looked to be a long way off. So did the actual day, but we needed to save up for it!

We decided to have our wedding on a Wednesday to cut the cost in half, and the 12/12/12 date honored the night we met, August 12. The ceremony would begin at 8:12 pm allowing plenty of time for a pre-ceremony cocktail hour, and while we weren't sure, we assumed a lot of people might need a drink. This would be the first time most of our guests would attend a gay wedding, even we had only been to one other.

Feeling that we were pioneers in marriage equality, we sent out invitations to 70 friends. Surprisingly and almost magically, the world changed before our eyes. Almost like a blink. You might not have taken much note of it, but on May 6, 2012, Vice President Joe Biden went on *Meet The Press* supporting gay marriage. Three days later, so did President Barack Obama. People were calling it "the defining issue of our day." On July 11th, CNN anchor Anderson Cooper came out of the closet, and in October 2012 my old friend and weather colleague Sam Champion announced his own engagement to his partner for New Year's Eve! In the November election that year, four new states—Maine, Minnesota, Maryland, and Washington—all voted to allow marriage for whoever wanted to marry. The equality door seemed to be swinging wide open just in time for our big day!

So, we couldn't just talk about it. We had to get going. Now, I completely understand how a $300 billion global industry revolves around weddings. It's almost easier to build a house. First, we had to pick colors: navy and silver. But from there, my gosh, did we want the round tables for six or for ten, and did we prefer the chairs "as is" or covered? If so, what color, and did we want cotton tablecloths or the silk tablecloths or the silk cloths with the trim or the silk cloths with the embroidery? And did we want those in navy with white napkins or those in silver with navy napkins? And that's just to put a cloth on a table with some chairs! The silverware, plates and glassware still all had to be chosen. Candles, votives, candelabras? Flowers—big flowers in small square vases, or small flowers in large tall vases, or just small all around so people could see each other?

Kevin, Morgan, and I at our own wedding in New York City, 2012.

Sylvia Weinstock, the lady with the big black round glasses, is a world-renowned cake maker who has made cakes for well-known people from Oprah, Robert De Niro, J.Lo, and Kim Kardashian to the Kennedys and Clintons. A cake from her was included in our wedding deal, fortunately, and she helped us choose a simple vanilla and chocolate cake decorated with bowties and bluebonnets, the state flower of Texas. Yellow roses, another Texas touch, would be at the tables. Dr. Terry Todd, a long-time Birmingham pal and Episcopal priest who teaches religious studies at a New Jersey college, kindly agreed to officiate.

The plan was simple 1) cocktail hour, 2) ceremony, and 3) dinner. The cocktail soirée would feature a drink we concocted of vodka, club soda, and pomegranate juice, which we nicknamed "The Skinny Groom" in a nod to the obligatory wedding-diet Kevin and I started months before. Dinner featured our favorites: cream of squash soup and short ribs, a good way to crater the diet.

As much fun, or frustration, as the party-planning was, we wanted the main feature to be the ceremony itself. For hours, I pored over marriage ceremonies from every religious and non-religious base, from all around the world. We wanted a traditional marriage, and we wanted our guests to witness a traditional wedding. Although gay marriage was new to all of us, we wanted our family and good friends coming away saying, "What a beautiful ceremony!"

As I became more familiar with the practices of different faiths, countries, cultures, and histories, I began to see commonalities. What *do* the people of the world consider most important as the very foundation of commitment? Basically, I discovered: I love you, you love me, let's build a life.

Amid the traditional "do you take" and "with this ring," we asked our friend Alice Melott from Galveston to read from the 2004 Massachusetts Supreme Court ruling on marriage equality as a subtle reminder that getting down this aisle had been a hard-knock road that was still being paved. We didn't take the privilege of getting married for granted.

The number 12 played a symbolic role besides the dates: 12 is a completing number in both religion and government. Just as there were 12 disciples and 12 tribes of Israel, so are there 12 jurors and 12 months in our calendar. The ability to be joined both spiritually and legally was an aspect of the ceremony that we wanted to highlight.

To include our religious heritages, Kevin's sister read scripture from Corinthians. And our son, Morgan, recited Robert Fulghum's poem "Unity." Fulghum, a born and bred Texan, wrote the book *All I Really Need to Know*

I Learned in Kindergarten. His simple philosophy in "Unity" captures why people who have been together a long time feel it's important to step over the line into a full commitment of marriage. A few of our friends had questioned why Kevin and I felt it was so necessary to take this extra step after spending 17 years together, and I wanted them to hear that poem.

For the venue, we chose Kimpton's Eventi Hotel in the Flower District of Manhattan. The first thing we noticed about those New Yorkers was how sincerely supportive and happy they are when people marry, no matter who is getting hitched. They even asked us to be on the hotel's website under "Real Weddings."

And soon it became very real. Guests rolled in for the rehearsal dinner the night before, and we all took a limo-bus down to Tribeca for Italian food and lots of wine, followed by a night out at a club called *Therapy*, which seemed appropriate for anyone the night before a lifetime commitment.

For years, I had received calls from brides-to-be and their mothers asking in August what the weather would be the following June. I had always been nice to them, but now I found myself in their proverbial bridal slippers. Thankfully, the weather turned out to be spectacular the whole week—crisp and sunny—no snow issues or storm delays. We all suited up to the nines with black tie and pretty dresses and the hotel's fourth floor transformed into the perfect spot.

Weddings should be unforgettably magical. And ours was. All the angst over the music, the drinks, the wine, the food, the decorations, the flowers, the seating chart, the ceremony, the readings, and the speeches came together in one quiet, winter evening in Manhattan, complete with tears, laughter and love.

The only thing missing had been our parents, all facing their own health issues. They said traveling to New York in winter was too much. A Texas wedding might have solved that problem, but we hadn't wanted to press them. As clearly as we feel their love, I would be lying if I said they completely understood and approved of what we were doing at the time. But our sisters were there, and plenty of other dear relatives and friends. Perhaps not having our parents there, and not needing to focus on the logistics of getting four seniors around the city, allowed us to be fully present to the ceremony and the guests.

I wondered at the time if my biological family would have felt differently—not just attending and enjoying, but even helping to plan. Maybe it wouldn't even have been their first gay wedding. Thoughts of all my parents, their known and unknown reactions to this major milestone in my life, added a touch of bittersweet that made the whole experience seem even more significant, if that were possible.

Then, there had been the fear factor. Although the grooms had left Houston, Houston came to us.

At three o'clock the afternoon of the wedding, Kevin and I had just returned to the Eventi from the Empire State Building, where we had been enjoying the incredibly mild, sunny afternoon. My friend and colleague Ryan Korsgard came into the room and announced, "I need pictures of you two. They're putting this on the news." Ryan's a terrific amateur photographer and even better professional reporter.

"Who needs pictures?" I asked. I had specifically requested that all the guests tone down the social media.

"Channel 2!" Ryan said, lifting his camera.

All smiles at our legal ceremony.

"*Our* Channel 2?" Ryan must have seen my eyes widen. My viewers knew me as a pretty authentic guy, but were they ready for this one? Spreading our wedding all over the airwaves? Was I ready?

We were about to find out. Although I had never hidden the fact that I was gay, I never thought it was of interest or import to anyone except my family and friends. I was in the glass closet; I knew people had called me the local Anderson Cooper. It wasn't a secret; but perhaps having hidden the fact as a young man, or perhaps because of my father's warning to be careful in the historically traditional South, I had never wanted to cause any waves. The people who knew, knew; the people who didn't—well, I thought they probably didn't care.

I had always felt the support from Channel 2, but I was surprised, and touched, that they wanted to share. Then I realized that my colleague, sportscaster Chester Pitts, had gotten married the day before. He had played football for the Texans for eight years, and the station had made a splash about his proposal and his big wedding. With that in mind, covering our marriage seemed more like a family decision than a business decision: *we covered Chester's story, so it's only right we cover Frank's.* But in the moment when Ryan lifted his camera, I didn't know whether to be more shocked or proud to have my Channel 2 family support me this way.

I do know it added yet another special aspect to a day that seemingly could not become more special. It was a brave step for them to share our marriage with the viewing public. Before Facebook became so universal, it was a big deal to share such personal information—and a modern, loving, thoughtful, right-thing-to-do deal. When I later thanked Emily Barr, the head of the broadcast division, she merely said, "Think nothing of it." But I knew most of my television viewers back home in Houston might need to take a deep breath.

I spilled my wine, one woman emailed me about hearing the news on TV that night. *Unbelievable, but I am really proud that Channel 2 had the guts to announce your wedding. And I'm really happy for you.*

Not so with everyone. Our assignment desk took one irate call: "How can you announce something like that? On TV?! Two *men* getting married, and you didn't even give us a warning to get our children out of the room!"

From dropped jaws to raised glasses, the public reaction ran the gamut. I had 5,000 Facebook friends—as many as are allowed on Facebook—and when our wedding went public, I instantly lost 500 of them. Disappointing, but not shocking. Another 5,000 people sent friend requests, and that meant a lot. We heard from newspapers and Internet sites wanting interviews, and through different news outlets around the country and the world, news of our wedding went viral.

A few weeks after our out-and-proud wedding, Kevin stood alone in a Home Depot line. One of the cashiers frantically waved him to her register. When he got there, her arms opened for a big hug.

"Thank you, thank you!" she said. "I know *exactly* who you are from your wedding being on the news, and you saved our family! You really did." Still patting on him, she went on to explain, "My niece and her female partner got married, and it was just tearing the family apart. When everyone found out about you two, and saw you on TV—well, it just seemed to make a lot of them understand. So thank you so much." We even heard from a local rabbi, inspired by us to come out to his entire synagogue.

Our wedding reached all kinds of families, many facing their own fears and questions as they watched their sons and daughters, nieces and nephews, best friends and college roommates fall in love with people of the same gender. Those folks also needed a little empathetic support to understand that they weren't alone in trying to get their head around the whole thing. Sometimes, being in the public eye gives me an opportunity to teach.

I didn't know if I would feel differently once we were married, but I did. Even though we'd been together since 1995, marriage is our society's natural conclusion to what we started when we first had met that August night in JR's Bar and Grille so many years before. I felt the joy of love, the seriousness of signing on the dotted line, and the relief of the future. Most importantly, as I had hoped our ceremony would convey, we now proudly stood as a family, legally and completely.

And with my marital status now a viral news item around the world, I figured when I found my new DNA relatives, especially the really close ones, they would likely Google me and find out pretty quickly that I married Kevin. There would be no surprises. No awkward having to come out to anyone ever again. No is-he-or-isn't-he curiosity.

Coming out to both my parents and my viewers, I had experienced the powerful force of curiosity. Followed to its natural conclusion—investigation and answers—it can unleash very unexpected results. After our wedding, everyone knew my personal truth. Kevin and I added a branch to the known part of my family tree, and we could not have been happier.

My personal life had taught me much about the force of curiosity—the lengths we will go to know the truth. My professional life also gave me more opportunity to experience it than you might expect. When it comes to weather, Mother Nature makes us all very curious, and she can get very personal. I found this out firsthand, in the most unexpected way.

5

REALITY TELEVISION STORMS IN

Curiosity truly is at the core of our existence. Just think, if Columbus hadn't been curious, we still might think the Earth was flat. As homo sapiens, trying to discover what lies beyond the current boundaries of our reality is a defining part of who we are. With rare exception, even the most dedicated ostriches determined to keep their heads in the sand will eventually succumb to curiosity. I had seen it personally, and in 2008 a major weather event slammed me with this understanding again: no matter how painful our discoveries might be, we are compelled to seek the truth.

Most of the country doesn't remember much about Hurricane Ike, because the very same weekend a bigger tsunami called "Lehman Brothers" flooded our financial world. The dire prophesies about the catastrophic impact of this financial storm turned out to be quite accurate. Worries and wonder were appropriate: the country would literally be left to hang out and dry alone. But no matter the severity of the economic forecast and the country's consuming interest in it, the weather kept coming.

"This is our storm," I told the producers three days before Hurricane Ike hit. At first, this monster storm, at times bigger than the devastating Hurricane Katrina had been, looked to have its sights set well south of Houston, but that changed. "All the models are converging now on Southeast Texas, not South Texas. Warm water is fueling the storm and SLOSH models are frightening."

SLOSH stands for Sea, Lake, and Overland Surges from Hurricanes. Imagine taking your arm to the back of a bathtub and pushing all the water toward the front, in a bathtub as big as the Gulf of Mexico. That surge was headed toward us. In real terms, it meant nightmare flooding.

"How high are we talking?" my news director asked.

"Twenty feet of water is possible," I told him. "Galveston Island will be under water." The possibility, so horrifying, was so real. Galveston sits along the coast, 27 miles long and three miles wide, protected somewhat by a 16 foot seawall built after the Great Storm of 1900. But that wall didn't extend to the west end of the island. "The west end could be gone. Bolivar Peninsula, just to the north, also."

And in the early morning hours of Saturday, September 13, 2008, Hurricane Ike drove directly into us with winds of 110 mph and a tidal surge of 12 to 21 feet of seawater, decimating the Bolivar Peninsula, just a ferry ride north of Galveston. When the waters receded, the piers and shops on Galveston's Gulf side were reduced to piles of sticks and debris, mounded with hundreds of boats now dry-docked in the middle of the road. Because of the storm's path, the island took a double hit of water—first from the south and then from the bay waters to the north. On the east end, the flood waters rose nine feet. The galleries, the restaurants, the homes, the businesses, all lay in utter disarray. Mud and debris littered everything that remained standing.

The permanent residents had been forced to leave before the storm. Now, the next day, that Sunday, they were barred from coming back. The island had no electricity, sewer, or water, and there were gas leaks, snakes, and nails everywhere. Right away, the local media went to work. But we quickly discovered that we were not allowed on the West End of the island, not even by helicopter. And none of the authorities would tell us why. Our helicopter pilots kept calling the Federal Aviation Administration (FAA) and asking why. Why were we not allowed to get information to our viewers?

By the end of Sunday, the curiosity and rumors spiraled out of control: Were dead bodies floating everywhere? Had the West End been wiped out like Bolivar Peninsula? Coast Guard Black Hawk helicopters flew, patrolling the beach like sharks. The FAA continued to ground all media. Were they hiding something? No one knew, and no one talked. Something, we assumed, must be going on.

On Monday, two things happened. First, Wall Street gave up and America's financial world raised a white flag, so the rest of the nation suddenly took no interest in our hurricane troubles down in Texas. If we expected the cavalry to ride in and rescue us, we were wrong. Caught up in our own storm, none of us realized the seriousness of the collapsing stock market and tumbling economy. We were not on anyone's to-do list.

Second, our KPRC News helicopter pilot decided to stop waiting for information and make something happen. Rather than peppering the stone wall that the FAA had become with calls and questions, he took the initiative to call TRACON (Terminal Radar Approach Control Facilities), the airport tower that handles local air traffic such as police and news helicopters and small private planes. They had wrested back control of the air space over Galveston and gave us permission to fly and photograph.

No other news outlets thought to call TRACON. We now had an exclusive fly-over to show that 1) there were no bodies floating around and 2) the West End survived, although it was in bad shape. From inside the helicopter, we aired live footage showing mountains of sand completely hiding the streets, hundreds of light poles snapped in half, roofs peeled back, decks demolished, windows blown out, garages underneath the homes hammered, and debris scattered everywhere. Amazingly, for the most part, the homes stood. They had not been obliterated.

My inbox back at the station began filling up with hundreds of emails inspired by our flight. The information highway had come to a dead end and people were beside themselves wanting to know more. All of them had the same running theme: *What does my house look like? Did you happen to* *fly over <u>this</u> neighborhood or <u>that</u> marina or <u>our</u> street? Please let me know!* The curiosity was killing them.

I went to my bosses with a plan: "We've got to get in the helicopter and fly back over the West End, get callers live on the phone with me, have them direct us to <u>their</u> homes, and show them their house in real-time. It's what everyone wants to see. I have hundreds of emails from people who just want to know what they are personally up against when they get home."

My news director loved the idea, and we got cracking. I rang up Alice Melott, my life-long friend who was a Galveston Realtor and had evacuated during the storm. I needed her help. Alice came to the station that Wednesday morning, and at the same time we revealed our plans to viewers: *I will be flying LIVE over the West End all afternoon. Send us your address, name, and phone number, and when we are in your neighborhood we will call you and have you direct us to your home so that we can show you the impact from the air.*

The emails flew into the station, and we printed them out. Alice, being thoroughly knowledgeable in the geography of the island, sorted the emails by community. I headed to the helicopter and climbed in, my pilot to the right, me on the left with headphones and microphone, and my photographer in the back to operate the zoom camera. By early afternoon we were in place.

The beating *whirrrrr* of the helicopter blades thumped like a metronome in the background. The sky, like most after a hurricane, burst in a brilliant teal-blue and the air felt cool. In the seat next to the chopper pilot, in my Ray-Ban sunglasses, red Channel 2 cap, and white polo shirt, I'm sure that I looked more like a traffic reporter than a TV weatherman, but for the next several hours I had been thrown into the role of an in-the-air over-the-air psychologist.

I am still amazed we pulled it off. Even with today's technology, communication is not quite real time. Just like a cellphone, there was a slight delay between the caller speaking and when I heard them; and here we had calls coming into our newsroom and getting patched through to me in the helicopter via a satellite dish, then me speaking to the callers and then the callers directing us where to go to see their houses. And just like the audio delay, there was a camera response delay. We had a lot of, "Turn the camera right, no, now left, no, back right a little bit." But somehow we managed. Our helicopter pilot hovered and turned and jogged, slightly back and forth and back again, with a surgeon's precision skill, and we somehow found those homes.

"Hi, Bob," I said to our first viewer. "We are over your neighborhood. What color is your house?" We needed that easy clue, as houses on the West End are usually a pastel green, blue, yellow, peach, or even gray and white. With the clear, blue sky, we could see for miles.

Bob directed us to his house, a blue-gray home that had quite literally fallen sixteen feet off its pilings, the thick poles meant to hold it up, safe from flooding. Ike had flattened Bob's house. As we zoomed tighter, it looked like Godzilla had strolled through the neighborhood. Bob's voice shook as he directed us.

"Oh, my. Oh, my, oh, my," he kept repeating.

"It doesn't look good, Bob. I'm so sorry," I said.

"Oh, it looks like it's in bad shape. I don't think I can save it."

We zoomed the camera in to Bob's flattened home and saw that he was right. Hurricane Ike's steel surge of water had left its mark, and I'm sure he wasn't able to save it. The stories from each caller sounded similar, but, thankfully, not all their homes were lost.

"It looks pretty good," one man said about his house. "Can you swing your helicopter around to the other side?" I laughed and thought we must be making our viewers pretty comfortable if they were going to start giving us directions. We spent all afternoon and into early evening flying over Galveston's West End, so much so that we had to refuel twice. We showed about 40 viewers their homes, talked to them about what we were all seeing for the first time, and tried to comfort them when the damage looked really serious. Truly, reality television at its most raw. No rehearsals, no fake arguments, no petty remarks—a Category Two hurricane had just wiped out much of our community, and we presented it live and uncensored: *Hurricane Ike: This is Your Life Now.*

Some homes had a side or roof torn away, but others seemed to have weathered the storm pretty well. From our angle we could only show a garage door buckled in, not the loss of everything in the garage. But we showed enough homes that, even if we didn't get to every last one, people got a sense of what they would be facing when they returned. Knowing what happened brought an enormous sense of relief, whether the consequences were dire or just inconvenient.

Weatherman-as-community-psychologist is a role I have played through the years in different ways. When Huricane Rita had aimed at us in 2005, I was the first on-air meteorologist who said this might turn and miss us. I had seen a model that was consistent with this outcome, and instinct and experience told me that Houston might be spared that time. Only three weeks earlier, everyone had seen Katrina demolish New Orleans. We still had evacuees in Houston! Tens of thousands tried to leave the city, stuck in a nightmare of 5 mph traffic. I did not send Kevin away and Hurricane Rita did turn to the north.

I had seen, time and again, how important it was to keep a level head in serious weather. When I relayed the news of the storm's changing path, I gave viewers their first glimmer of hope. I understood then that for someone like me who people see everyday in their homes, the psychologist role is necessary when we are faced with that kind of a threat. After Hurricane Rita, I even had one woman tell me, "You need to be the governor of this state."

Hurricane Ike occurred in 2008, and since then the East Coast has experienced its own slaughter from Hurricane Sandy. We've had other tropical threats and floods here in Houston, but, remarkably, to this day I still meet people who want to talk to me about that one afternoon when I flew over the island to show people their damaged homes. On so many different levels that day turned out to be good journalism and interesting to watch; but, on the most basic level, I satisfied the curiosity tormenting us. People have a serious relationship with their homes—not just financial, but emotional. Home is where family happens.

I have seen—and experienced—that not knowing something that you really want to know about your home or family can plunge you so deeply into your emotions that when you do find the answers, you never forget from when and where those answers came. Those Ike Flights continue to be my proudest moment as a television weatherman, but they also brought to me the true meaning of "needing to know" and "holding out hope," which are two maxims in family searches.

We all know the story of Pandora's box, but most people don't remember the full story. Yes, Pandora's curiosity got the best of her and she opened the box releasing a myriad of evils to the world. Yet what is often overlooked is that Hope did not escape—it was somehow left in the bottom of the box. The ancient Greeks understood that no matter the pain of life, without hope there is nothing.

If the Ike discoveries taught me more about curiosity, they also should have warned me that sometimes we find more than we are looking for. I had plenty of hope on this new DNA journey, but I wasn't aware that other things would have to come out of the box first. As the first bits of information began coming in, they hit me like the initial waves of a major hurricane. The first big breakthrough would come on Valentine's Day, of all days.

6

Y IN THE WORLD

After a cold snap the day before, the sun shone and the February day warmed to the upper 70s—the kind of let's-go-golfing-in-winter day we Houstonians brag about while snow mountains pile up in Boston. The dogs and I were checking emails on the love seat in the kitchen, when a message from Morgan Hawthorne came up on the screen.

Can you call me?!?! As we all do, I anticipated that Valentine's Day would be a special day, but Morgan was not the person I was expecting to surprise me. *Your results are in and they are amazing! Make sure you are by a computer so I can explain them to you.*

I popped up, dumping the dogs and my computer into the soft pillows. I scrambled around trying to find my phone, surprised by how energized I was by her short message. My stomach was doing little flips, telling me to hurry and call her.

Six weeks earlier, when I had sent in the sample, I had the sensation I was stepping off a cliff. The process itself was unremarkable: I had taken the small scrapers, like a cross between a toothbrush and a Q-Tip®, brushed firmly inside my cheek and placed my DNA in the vial. But then I realized what I was about to do.

"OK," I said to myself, surprised I needed any self-coaching at this point. "I'm going to do this. It's time to spit or get off the pot." Why was I even thinking about it? Was I going to do all this phone-calling and research, but not actually send in the DNA sample? "I have nothing to lose," I thought with conviction, and I sent the package back to Family Tree DNA (FTDNA) before I hesitated again.

And then I waited. It takes so long because of the 3 billion pieces of DNA code; 750,000 pieces of information called SNPs ("snips") are counted. This is as much as you need to be able to determine relationships. The technical term for a SNP is a single nucleotide polymorphism, but that's more than most of us want to know. Once your vial arrives at the labs of FTDNA, it is logged into their computer system. Then the sample undergoes a separation with a very fancy and expensive machine that separates the DNA cells from all the rest of your cells (saliva, for instance). That "pure DNA" is logged into the computer system where it is compared to the DNA of everyone else who is in the system, and the results are eventually posted.

You are then able to log on and see all of your results and find out how many other people match your DNA and to what extent. I have learned that all of the DNA testing companies use pretty much the same protocol for sampling and measuring. The biggest difference is that *Ancestry.com* and *23andMe.com* have you spit in a tube, rather than scrape.

While I was waiting for my results, Morgan had invited me for a tour of the offices and labs of FTDNA. They take up the entire 8th floor of a building on the north side of Houston.

"It's a little like Silicon Valley," I told her, not that I'd ever been to Silicon Valley. The office side reminded me of what a university study hall must look like these days—a lot of young faces with a myriad of computer screens. There are few cubicles, mostly just desk after desk. I'm not sure I even saw any phones on the desks—I guess everyone is on their cell. And just like all the high-tech companies you hear about, dress is casual, free lunch is served on Fridays, and you bring your smarts, savvy, and hard work to the game.

With Bennett Greenspan, founder of Family Tree DNA in Houston.

The lab takes up the other half of the space, pristine and clean with techs in white coats making sure all the vials of DNA are properly placed, set, analyzed, and stored. Morgan told me there are literally tens of thousands of vials coming in every month. Properly cataloguing, testing, and sending out the results takes time. Quality assurance is primo. The turnaround time simply makes sense.

While there, I had met the CEO of the whole place, Bennett Greenspan, who beamed as he presented me with one of the company's gray T-shirts. It asks the simple question on the front: *What's in Your Genes?* I have to admit I like bad puns.

And now the moment arrived: Morgan's email. Everyone complains about emails not delivering the right tone, but this one sounded absolutely breathless with excitement. When I got through to her, she still sounded excited. Not only were the DNA results finally back, they were back with enough information to actually make the folks at Family Tree DNA take particular notice. That had to be a good sign! I held my breath.

"We are all so excited!" Morgan exclaimed. "It's all the office is talking about! Mind you, not everyone gets *these* kind of results!" It sounded like my Colonial Soup had been poured from a very large and important pot. I could tell from her voice that I had hit some kind of DNA lottery. What could it mean, getting these kinds of results? "Have you logged in to your account?" she asked.

"Just a second," I said. My heart skipped beats, and my hands were sweaty just getting the computer turned on.

"Okay, first, let's go over the Y-DNA which you got directly from your biological father. Open that and tell me what you see," Morgan said, sounding like a patient teacher. She's like that, but I knew she was raising a two-year-old. Instruction is second nature to her by now. "There's a lot to absorb and this can be confusing at first."

No kidding. I looked. "I see 37 names with numbers by them, 0s and 1s and 2s and 3s and 4s. Each name has a number. What does that mean?" I'm sure Morgan rolled her eyes at that point.

"I'll get to that. What *name* do you see?" she asked. Of course! Man after man after man—all of whom shared my DNA—had a running theme for a last name: Hensley. One Henslee, but I have learned since that last name spelling variations really mean nothing. I noted that Hen-sley and Billing-sley were remarkably similar—solid Englishman names! Fee-fi-fo-fum!

"So," I started cautiously. I had it figured out, but didn't want to sound stupid. "Does this mean I am a "Hensley" by blood? For *certain?*" I had to verify it. There I sat on the edge of my corduroy couch, 54 years old and finding out for the first time that my heritage is shared with all the Hensleys of the world. Had I ever even heard this name before?

"Yes, you have to be a Hensley. Count how many Hensleys there are on both pages," she replied.

GENETIC DISTANCE	NAME		MOST DISTANT ANCESTOR
0	C**** Hensley	Y-DNA37 FF	Samuel Hensley, b. 1664 and d. 1734
0	Mr. ****** ******* Hensley	Y-DNA37	
0	Mr. R****** Hensley Sr.	Y-DNA37	Harmon Hensley b 1799 d 1835
0	Mr. Mark Brown {adopted} Hensley	Y-DNA67 FF	
0	D***** D***** Hensley	Y-DNA37	
0	W****** W******* Henslee	Y-DNA67	
1	C***** R** Hensley	Y-DNA67	L. W. Hensley, 1849 -

GENETIC DISTANCE	NAME		MOST DISTANT ANCESTOR
1	N***** W***** Hensley	Y-DNA67 FF	James Hensley b 1777/8 Virginia
1	C***** H******* Hensley	Y-DNA37	
1	McCallister		James McCallister, b.c. 1755, VA
1	D****** R** Hensley	Y-DNA67 FF	James Hensley, 1605
1	J** K. Hensley	Y-DNA37	Hensley
1	Mr. G******** Coe	Y-DNA37	Luther Edward Coe (Hensley)
1	L****** V** Henslee	Y-DNA37	
1	C******* Hensley	Y-DNA67	Allen Hensley b. 1818 TN d. 1870-1880 KY
1	B***** W***** Hensley	Y-DNA37	Benjamin Hensley
1	Calhoun	Y-DNA37	
1	Mr. K** Hensley	Y-DNA67	CTedes Hensley, 1793, NC
1	Mr. G*** Hensley	Y-DNA67	Fielding Hensley b. 1762 Buckingham Co., Va. D. 18
2	McCallister	Y-DNA37	James McCallister, b.c. 1755 VA
2	J***** T***** Hensley	Y-DNA67	James Hensley, b 16 Sept 1818, KY
2	Mr. F***** J***** Hensley I	Y-DNA37	William HENSLEY, b.1583 and d. 1654
2	M****** L** Hensley	Y-DNA67 FF	John Hensley, 1803-1882
2	Mr. G****** H****** Hensley	Y-	Benjamine Hensley, 1776-1850

I counted and counted again. "28 of 36," I said.

"That is more than enough, but we only tested to 37 markers."

"So much terminology, I thought." "Remind me, what's a marker?"

"Basically, a closer look at how much DNA you match. The more markers we look at, the more significant matches we can find. We want to upgrade you to 67 markers. This will be even more deterministic," Morgan assured me.

I still had no idea what markers meant or what they did, but clearly the more markers FTDNA counts, the more they know. I made a general OK-go-on sound, and she continued.

"Those numbers on the far left—the 0s, 1s, 2s 3s—are how close you are genetically to each man. So at 0, we call that a 37/37 marker match and you certainly share a distant relative, probably no more than a few generations back."

"So if a generation is 30 years, then you mean 120 years ago?" I asked. That seemed like a very long time ago. How could they find my biological parents from that far back? She had obviously explained this process before, because she answered before I could ask.

"Yes, but this is how we get your family tree going. We need to see how many matches you'll get if we count 67 markers." Then Morgan's voice became a little more excited. "And have you noticed the fourth man, down?"

I had. Mark Brown. Another adoptee. A Hensley adoptee, just like me!

"Yes, are you thinking the same thing I'm thinking?" I asked. How strange would that be… a Hensley man having two sons out in the world, both put up for adoption.

"Mark is adopted also, so who knows? Perhaps the same Hensley man is father to you both. You may be half brothers," Morgan suggested.

A half brother! "How can we tell?" I asked, already wondering if he looked like me, or if he was interested in theater. What if he were a weatherman?

"We can't from the Y-DNA. We really need to ask Mark to upgrade to the Family Finder test. If you share 35-50% of DNA, you are brothers. 25% and you are half brothers!"

I immediately searched Facebook for Mark Brown only to realize there were thousands of men named "Mark Brown."

"I can't Google him, Morgan. Can you reach out to him?" I asked.

"I'll see if we can get Mark to agree to a Family Finder test, which will compare your primary DNA, not just the Y you got from your fathers," she said. "To figure out if Mark and you are truly closely related, the Family Finder is a must. I'll shoot him an email." It was an easy sell after all, as people who take the DNA tests are eager to find family themselves.

Mark agreed within minutes, and we immediately ordered the upgrade to Family Finder, which would compare the other 22 chromosomes. There are costs involved in each test, usually a hundred or so dollars each, and they can add up. But for the people who want to satisfy the curiosity of a lifetime, the cost is usually not a deterrent.

We crossed our fingers to see what would happen! Two years younger than me, Mark was born in New Jersey and adopted from there. Both his adoptive parents had passed away, and now he searched for biological family. Morgan sent me what picture she had of him: dark eyes and hair, far from my blue eyes and dirty blonde hair; but we agreed that DNA doesn't lie, and there's the simple chance that our "playing cards" were from the same deck, just slightly different. We could easily share the same father.

And a "Chuck Hensley" also happened to be a distant match, as well. His profile included his Hensley Family Tree to nine generations. I found out quickly with a little Googling that Chuck had a fourth great-grandfather, William Richardson Hensley, whose good friend Travis B. Austin died at the Alamo. This William Hensley fought in the Battle of San Jacinto.

I knew that I also had a Billingsley ancestor who fought for Texas independence. Captain Jesse Billingsley had a best friend: none other than Davy Crockett. Jesse's direct descendants live near Houston, and they had proved through letters of the day that Jesse was the person who came up with the slogan "Remember the Alamo!" He shouted this battle cry on behalf of Davy at the Battle of San Jacinto, just six weeks after the Alamo fell. I had Googled to make sure, and the Texas Legislature did indeed credit Captain Jesse Billingsley with those famous words.

Chuck Hensley and I most likely share a common relative back to five generations, 150 years or more. William Richard Hensley showed up six generations back, so within that time frame we are related, but the mere idea that I would be on his Hensley tree and that my adoptive Jesse Billingsley fought side by side in battle with him sent me to the moon!

"Remember the Alamo" is a big deal in Texas. In fact, I told Jesse's story once on TV and immediately got an email from a viewer offering me membership in an exclusive descendants' club. I quickly confessed that, being adopted, I didn't share the Billingsley bloodline, and that ended that. But suddenly I knew that I was a Hensley, and the Hensleys were there at those battles, too!

Despite being given membership in the Billingsley club when Pat and Jimmy took me as their own, in some ways I was just a sort-of-member, like an honorary member. I knew I had a family, but I didn't have a genetic heritage. I couldn't take "blood pride" in those who came before me, so I had always convinced myself that it didn't matter.

Suddenly, it all seemed different. From one little swab of cheek, and the miracles of modern science, I had now discovered that there was a club where I was a full member. Members of my club, or at least one of them, had fought at the Alamo.

And my clubhouse was fixing to get a lot bigger.

7

THE FRANK CLUB:
COOL KIDS ONLY

If you think the Hensley forefather, ferociously and fearlessly, fighting alongside the Billingsley forefather turned out to be just an easy coincidence, you might be right. After all, those Hensleys and Billingsleys all boated over from England in the same century, all part of that Colonial Soup. But knowing about it made me eager to know more, in a way I would not have thought possible based on the dismissive, and probably defensive way, I had dealt with the concept of ancestors before.

Someone in 1936 put together a book called *The Billingsley Family in America*.

"Your daddy is in this book," my Great-aunt Renna, the family genealogist, told me.

"Really?" I said, politely. "That's cool." And I smiled. These stories always impressed me. Yet, in the back of my mind, I categorized these stories of past Billingsley generations as merely interesting, but obviously not my stories. They weren't really *my* generations. Not my club.

"Right here!" she pointed. I saw my dad, Jimmy, right there, 11th generation down the line. I could see he went right back to John and Amanda Billingsley who left England in 1620 to escape religious persecution. "They were Quakers who went to Holland, and they had five sons who all came to America in 1640. They moved to Virginia. Francis Billingsley was the only son to have more sons; the rest died," she said. Aunt Renna looked at me earnestly. "So if you are a Billingsley in America, then you can thank Francis. All the Billingsleys go right back to him."

I did learn one important genealogical lesson from my Aunt Renna, quite by accident. I will never forget her insistence in those days that her Irish McBrides were related to President James K. Polk, which in her mind gave the family tree strong social roots. She would never know of anything called the Internet, but a little research turned up that our connection to the presidential line was a myth, started by a cousin named Polly Polk who lied to a magazine. No genealogical proof exists that Polly and James shared even one common ancestor.

As I revved up my family search, I kept this point in mind: family stories are sometimes just stories.

"DNA never lies," Morgan said after I told her this tale. We were on the phone reviewing the results of my upgraded search. "So let's look at Family Finder, the people you share the rest of your DNA with."

I clicked on that. Family Finder is the DNA test that measures our 23 chromosomes, pared down to more than 750,000 SNPs, or markers. The more SNPs, and the longer the strand of DNA that we share with someone, the stronger the relationship. You can think of the card analogy. Not only might we share the 8 of Diamonds, but if we have a running sequence of the 8-9-10 of Diamonds also, then it's an even stronger match.

"Whoa! There are 90 pages of matches with 25 people on each page!" I exclaimed.

Morgan slowed me down. "Yes, and you'll have great fun exploring that. But most of them are remote cousins—third to sixth cousins. You do have a fourth cousin, though, Janine Cloud, and guess what—she works right here at FTDNA!"

After a little discussion of that strange coincidence, Morgan walked me through the rest of the results, page by page. After our call, I was able to contact many of these newly discovered relatives by Facebook and email.

LISA JANINE CLOUD
Fourth Cousin – Remote Cousin

What's interesting is that Janine and I only share about .2% of DNA—a third cousin to fifth cousin—but her father and I share .4%, twice as much, which is what makes DNA so interesting. That card shuffle can recombine in so many different ways.

The coincidence of the day: "Look at that 12th name on the list!" Morgan pointed out.

MR. FRANK BILLINGSLEA
Second Cousin – Fourth Cousin

"You, adoptee whose name is Frank Billingsley, are cousins with a man who is also named Frank Billingslea!"

I would later send him an email: *Hi! We are distantly related and through my Y-DNA I am definitely a Hensley. However, I am adopted and my name is Frank Billingsley—and I am related to you and you are related to a Billingsley. Gotta love DNA! So I am guessing that somewhere along the line I AM actually a little Billingsley also! Can you tell me more about your Billingsley line?*

Frank Billingslea's daughter, who I also shared DNA with and who takes care of his account, wrote me back: *That is an amazing coincidence you are an adopted Billingsley. Frank Billingslea is my father and he did get your email as well, and I always respond for him. Our Billingslea line is from West Virginia and at one time our last name was spelled with -ley and not -lea. I do have a tree on Ancestry.com and will send you an invite to it. I have read the book and do remember your father in it. My grandfather, also, named Frank Billingslea was born in W Virginia and only came to Oklahoma b/c he was a driller and then became a producer. I am still amazed your name is Frank Billingsley.*

I compared Frank Billingslea's tree to Jimmy's, which I had thanks to Aunt Renna and her book. There they were: Frank's sixth great-grandfather and my dad, Jimmy's, seventh great-grandfather were brothers! Not only had my adopted and biological families fought side by side, I had just discovered this remote, but true relationship to my own adoptive father!

My dad's reaction was classic: "I always knew I picked right!" All this information had me beside myself. I really *am* a Billingsley! Somewhere! Maybe we all do go back to Francis!

ALICIA HALL
Third Cousin – Fifth Cousin

I also shared a mere .2% of DNA with a young lady named Alicia Hall. I have always been partial to the name "Alicia." After starting my career in the fall of 1982, Hurricane Alicia spun up as the first hurricane I ever talked about on TV, a storm that would take direct aim for Houston that August of 1983. In today's dollars, Alicia brought five billion dollars worth of damage and killed 21 people. Most Houstonians who went through it remember tons of glass shards falling from the newly built downtown sky-scrapers. That glass landed all over the streets and impaled car hoods like dartboards. At the time, I lived in Virginia and had never stepped foot in Houston, but that hurricane officially welcomed me into the world of pro-fessional weathercasting.

Now I had a new "Alicia" in my life. Alicia Hall certainly gave me my first welcome into the world of expert genealogy, although at first I honest-ly didn't give our meager share of DNA much thought. But *she* did, because that small .2% made me *her* highest match—and, somehow, I shared DNA with both her mother and her father. This made her very interested in *my* tree (even though my tree didn't exist just yet).

Alicia is a smart cookie, originally from Jamaica, now living in New York City and working for a life insurance company. She has traced her pa-ternal seventh great-grandmother all the way back to the Congo in Africa. Yes, Africa. Alicia is a gorgeous black woman. So now a Southern, white, weatherman in Houston, Texas, shows up as her strongest DNA match somehow related to *both* her parents? That definitely got her attention, and thank goodness for it! She would become my sounding board for all my family theories. Somewhere, we're cousins. Knowing what she did about DNA, she wasn't surprised at my being white. The shock was that I was related to both her mother and father. Talking the implications of this connection through with Alicia was a real wakeup call to me that we are all related. Racism is definitely taught.

My conversations with Alicia changed my understanding of how the people of the world relate and are related, but it was Bettyjean Kindall, the person on my Family Finder list with the strongest DNA connection, who changed everything for me personally.

8

X MARKS THE SPOT

BETTYJEAN KINDALL
First Cousin – Third Cousin
A 4% share of DNA! Just (barely) enough DNA to be a first cousin once removed! Here is a quick lesson on "once removed"—if your parent is the first cousin of someone, then you are that person's first cousin once removed (or one generation lower). You'd be second cousins with that person's child.

"So what does this 4% mean, exactly?" I asked Morgan as I began to search Facebook for a Bettyjean page.

"It's a lot of DNA to share, Frank. She's a close family member. We think she's at least a second cousin, meaning she has the same great-grandparents. But given your generational difference, there is every possibility that she is a first cousin once removed. That means that one of her grandparents is your great-grandparent." For instance, her grandmother might be my great-grandmother.

"That seems pretty remote," I said.

"Oh, but it's not. *And* she also shares the X chromosome with you."

"Which means?"

"She is on your mother's side. As a male, remember you always get your Y chromosome from your biological father—that's always father to father, male to male. So as a male, you can only get your X chromosome from your biological mother. For Bettyjean to share the X chromosome with you means she is definitely somehow related to your biological mother."

"So if I am a first cousin once removed… then my mother would be a first cousin of Bettyjean's?"

"Exactly."

I found her Facebook page.

Bettyjean looked like she came in from Central Casting as the little old lady from Pasadena, or in this case, Little Rock. My biological mother, supposedly 18 when she had me, would now be 72. My mother being a first cousin to Bettyjean definitely seemed possible.

"I just found her on Facebook," I told Morgan. Honestly, I couldn't believe she had a Facebook page, but she did, and a good 500 friends! "She's from Little Rock. She has to be a close relative." I enlarged the one and only picture. She had bright blue eyes, just like mine. She definitely had her go-to-meeting clothes on, and she appeared to be standing in a narthex or fellowship hall. Over her shoulder hung a portrait of Jesus, a young white man with a soft brown beard, very familiar to me from my childhood. I wondered why she took a selfie with Jesus. I zoomed the picture in to her big, brassy nametag and saw that it declared her a member of The Church of Jesus Christ Latter-day Saints.

"Oh, wow, Morgan," I said. "Bettyjean is a Mormon." I let that sink in for a minute. "I might be a Mormon?" I had assumed that all my relatives would be just like me. Now I had a black distant cousin and a Mormon second cousin. I was quickly getting more diverse. Elder Frank? My blue eyes and blonde hair were the perfect fit.

"Seriously?" Morgan squealed with a sheer happiness that only confused me. "That's wonderful!" She caught her breath. "You don't realize it, but if Bettyjean is a Mormon, you may have just hit the genealogical jackpot!"

I had no idea. A Mormon jackpot? What was she talking about?

Morgan explained, "Mormon genealogy is the most complete in the entire world."

What I didn't understand at the time was that Mormons *seal*, or "join eternally," family members, so that those familial relationships will last beyond death. Spouses are sealed to each other forever (it's not just until death do us part, it's for keeps); children are sealed to parents. And they seal all their relatives, whether those relatives are Mormon or not. And they don't ask, they just do it, which makes it a bit controversial. Mormons also *baptize* their dead relatives so that they may enter the Kingdom of Heaven, having the opportunity to accept or reject that baptism in the afterlife. Simply put, if your Mormon relative baptizes you, even if you are already dead, then God will approach you and offer you the chance to become a Mormon and get into Heaven. I'll let it rest there, but you can imagine how debatable this practice might be.

The upside for me was that I had stumbled on a genealogical treasure. In order to make sure everyone is sealed or baptized the Mormons have to know who everyone is, when they were born, when they died, who they married, the children they had. Records have to be kept! Lots and lots of records! It's a perfect scenario for a big family tree. There is no question that The Church of Jesus Christ Latter-day Saints in Salt Lake City houses the largest genealogical library in the world—more than two billion deceased names on file. One of those "places to visit before you die" because your name will likely be there eventually anyway, it has a huge collection of primary research tools, including federal and state census records, port rosters, naturalization records, county records, foreign civil registration records, tens of thousands of family histories, and thousands of maps. Genealogists who make this "trip to bountiful" usually return exhausted.

Morgan continued, "We need to find out if Bettyjean has her family tree and start looking. I feel your biological mother is somewhere on that tree." Morgan reasoned that if the relationship proved accurate, then I needed to take a close look at all of Bettyjean's female first cousins.

"Should I look on her mother's side or father's side?" I asked.

"Both. You can only get your X chromosome from your mother, but Bettyjean got both an X from her mother and an X from her father. So all her female first cousins on both sides are candidates to be your biological mother," she reasoned. That, of course, assumed that Bettyjean and I were first cousins once removed.

"What if she's a second cousin?" I asked.

"That is also possible and means you would share the same great-grand-parents. We can still follow the X chromosome and the way it is passed down the line. If we have a tree, we'll have names." Names! Always looking for names!

And, of course, one of those names would have to end up belonging to a female, probably born around 1942. And given that my birth happened in Little Rock, the woman likely lived in Arkansas in 1960. It was speculation, of course, but we had to start somewhere.

Bettyjean's FTDNA profile included her email address. What did we ever do before email? I already felt proud to be related to such a sweet-looking 80-year-old who had both a Facebook page and an email account! I sent her a valentine:

Today, I received the Family Finder results and you and I are first to third cousins—you, in fact, are my most direct match. I looked you up on Facebook and, well, I see that you are from Little Rock!! What a coincidence! I thought perhaps you could shed some light on my birth parents?? If you and I are first cousins then perhaps you might have an insight as to my Hensley father, or maybe my maternal line? Of course, any information about my family is welcome. I am new to all of this so any guidance you may have to offer is needed! By the way, I notice that you and I both have blue eyes! I even think we look alike.

Thanks so much for taking time to read this!

Frank

A 4% DNA share! My next highest match fell well under 1%. Bettyjean really measured up.

Right now I had three mysterious people on my tree, but I had a family tree for the first time in my life! Can you imagine? I knew people, sort of, whom I could call *relatives*. Not so much a tree, more a twig really, but mine!

Frank's Family Tree as of Valentine's Day 2014:

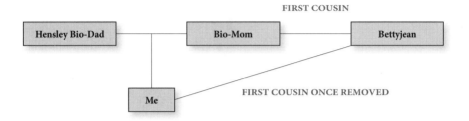

Cousin Bettyjean and Mysterious Mr. Hensley. She had the Facebook page, and she did have an email address, so she seemed tech-advanced, but I had no idea how long I would have to wait before she got around to checking email. And, if she did, would my note have gone to spam? I would give it a couple of days and then find a phone number.

Turns out, she answered me back in fifteen minutes.

"Are you a Hensley? I have one Hensley in my tree."

9

A VALENTINE'S
SWEETHEART

***B**ettyjean is a delightful, funny lady born in the early 1930s. She wrote a whole book on her family's genealogy back in the mid-1970s. In fact, she wrote 11 books while raising her family—a pretty high bar as I sit here on the couch with my dogs trying to write just one! So she became very interested in this new relationship, but understandably, cautious of me at first.

"No, I do not think we are related through the Hensley line. That's my father's line. I think you might be related to my biological mother," I explained.

"You aren't on my mother's line, the Baker line," she wrote, matter-of-factly. *"If you were, I would know about you. That's my Mormon side. Maybe you are on my father's Garland line. I will send you my pedigree,"* she said. "Pedigree" sounded more like something for a purebred cocker spaniel, but apparently it's just fancy

talk for a family tree. She sent me her pedigree for both her mother and father's side back five generations. It had names!

Since I know my X chromosome goes to Mom, and Bettyjean shared the X with me, a fact determined by the DNA test, then obviously she and bio-Mom were related—but where? Bettyjean's DNA match did not go high enough to be my aunt, so my mom wouldn't be her sister; in other words, they didn't share a parent. But *their* parents must have been brother and sister for them to be first cousins and for me to be a first cousin once removed. Those parents would go back to the same grandparents. Either the Garlands or the Bakers.

I called Morgan back when I heard from Bettyjean. Fortunately, there is a totally unrelated DNA test which Morgan ran for both me and Bettyjean. Called "mitochondrial" DNA, it's a distinct and separate molecule that doesn't change much over 10,000 years and is passed from mother to mother to mother. And, we found out shortly the best news yet: Bettyjean and I were *not* a match on this particular DNA, so that helped rule out being related on Bettyjean's mother's side—the Bakers, which turned out to be the Mormon side.

So we knew to search Bettyjean's dad Ollie's side, the Church of Christ side. That is where the matching X came from. Ollie could only have gotten his X from his mother, Pearl.

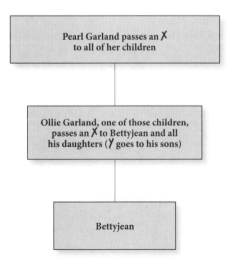

Bettyjean gets the X from father Ollie—she also got one from her mother, a Baker, but Morgan and I ruled that out as a direction for me to search.

And so did Bettyjean when I contacted her with the mitochondrial results. "You are *not* on my mother's line," she insisted again.

Certainly, her feeling was most likely true. Mormon children placed for adoption are, as a rule, placed with Mormon families. Today the families are actually interviewed by the birth mother before choosing where the baby will go. I had been placed with a Protestant couple. Bettyjean told me her father had been Church of Christ but converted to Mormonism when marrying her mother, whose uncle had founded the first Mormon Church in Arkansas.

Bettyjean continued, "You must be on my father's side, but still, I've never heard of you. If you were a secret, I don't want to be the one to stir the cauldron, so to speak."

I understood. I had been so caught up in the puzzle of DNA and genealogy, I hadn't given much thought to the cauldron heating up. Finding family members with secrets can certainly start a few fires. So, I didn't know if our email connection would end that day or not. Would Bettyjean be a best friend or a dead end? I pulled back a bit.

But I was also waiting now for Mark Brown's results, the other adopted Hensley. And I was working another angle, too: I had upgraded from 37 markers to 67 markers on the Y-DNA test. When these results came in, my family tree began to really branch out.

10

A FAMILY TREE GROWS IN MANHATTAN

"Your DNA seems to be scattered from a shotgun," Alicia declared. My cousin waits for nothing. We had become instant friends via email. She has a passion for genealogy and a brain that can put dates and people and places somewhere up in her mind's eye where she just "sees" it. There are no words to adequately describe her intuition. But she is fast and furious when she searches, and her gut is rarely wrong.

A month after my first DNA results came in, Alicia and I were digging to figure out our exact relationship. I had Googled early settlers with the name Hensley and discovered:

The exact period of settlement in North America has not been definitely determined, but information extracted from public and civil registry archives confirm that one of the first settlers was a certain "William Hensley," aged 40. He immigrated to

North America in 1774, sailing from the Port of Bristol aboard the ship named the "Charlotte Packet" on the 7th of November 1774, arriving in Jamaica on the 14th of November of the same.

Come on, Alicia. I'm sure once he got to Jamaica he felt really, really ready to meet the locals, I observed in one of my late night emails to her—despite the fact that his occupation listed him as Gentleman, whatever that really meant. *This same William Hensley eventually landed in America with several Jamaicans with him.* I tried to convince her that our genetic lines crossed somewhere between Montego Bay and the Delmarva Peninsula.

She didn't bite. It was too simple, and it didn't explain the connection being on both sides. Alicia's mission became to find out what she could about me, where I came from, and how we were related. She calls it the Frank Family Wagon.

Alicia knows her mother and father are not related in any way, and yet I show up as a distant cousin to them *both*? How in the world did *that* happen? As I write, we're still looking for that answer. Not a lot of Jamaican people have their DNA tested, and their genetic lines seem as mashed up as ackee and saltfish. We have also discovered a Hensley who was an American Revolution POW held in Jamaica... so...

Alicia turned her attention back to my search. *Ok, so we're looking at all of Pearl's children, the sons and daughters, because all of them would get an X from her. One of the children's daughters could be your mother. All of her children are possibilities.* One thing I can tell you about Arkansas farming families: they have a lot of children. I guess, in the day, there were a lot of rows to hoe.

So the line of thought seemed pretty simple: Pearl would be my great-grandmother. One of her children is my grandmother or grandfather, and one of their daughters is my mother.

So, we need to find ALL of Ollie's brothers and sisters and all of their daughters? I asked.

Yes, confirmed Alicia.

I'm going to reach out to Bettyjean again, I declared. I needed to be careful—I could tell Bettyjean knew how to keep a family secret. If she didn't want me exploring her family tree, then she would take an ax to it just like the State of Arkansas had. I sent her another email:

Hi Bettyjean,

Since we do share the X chromosome and I can only get that from my mother, then we must be related on my maternal side. I agree that I am not on your Baker side. Clearly, I am no genealogist—I have attached a chart indicating where our common ancestor might be. It would seem that on your father's side we would be related through your grandmother, Pearl Jones. Your father's mother. Is that the way you see this? Thanks again for your help and hope you are doing well!

Bettyjean replied, short and sweet: *The best way to answer is to send you my short pedigree.*

Wait—hold your horses! Hadn't she sent me her short pedigree already? There's more? Indeed. A lot more. Apparently, the first pedigree she sent read more like the *Reader's Digest* abridged version. I wondered why she had just thrown me that little bone at first.

I clicked the download she emailed which had an obsolete extension, originally exclusive to The Church of Jesus Christ Latter-day Saints (LDS). The download began and hummed away for a good two minutes. It was like watching a slot machine in Vegas turn and turn and turn until you hit that sweet triple 7s. But in this case it hit 13,523. Names. More names than I knew what to do with. To convert the old format, I used a popular genealogy program called RootsMagic that Morgan had told me about. It sorted everything by descendent, location, birth, death, LDS sealings, and LDS baptisms. I still find it so ironic that Mormon genealogical research solely designed to secure a good afterlife became my key to figuring out what had happened in my now-life.

I had, indeed, hit the Mormon jackpot, and I couldn't wait to cash in my winnings.

11

I HATE HOMEWORK

Two names stood out.

Pearl and Hank, Bettyjean's grandparents (and presumably my great-grandparents) had six children. Four boys and two girls.

I quickly ruled out the two girls—their daughters were already having other children in 1960 so they certainly couldn't have been having me as well.

That left the four boys:

- Son 1—Drew, died at age one, so he was out
- Son 2—Ollie, Bettyjean's Dad, would be my great-uncle
- Son 3—Adam, two daughters, the oldest born in 1945 would have been 15 at the time I was born—possible
- Son 4—Donald, four daughters, one born in 1940 and one born in 1943. They would have been 20 or 17 when I was born. Two other daughters would have been 30 and 33.

So, that narrowed it to Donald's youngest daughters or Adam's 15-year-old daughter (I would discover later there is an England, Arkansas). But, according to Bettyjean's tree, Adam's daughter was born in England. So if they had left the country, it seemed unlikely for her to be in Little Rock in 1960. Possible, but I learned quickly that when doing a search like this, it was best to home in on one thing at a time. So I focused on Donald's two youngest daughters:

- Beaulah—born in 1941, would have been 19 or maybe 18 1/2 in 1960
- Tanya—born in 1943, would have been 17 in 1960

Neither one would have been *exactly* 18 at my birth, but close. Anyone who has even a minute of studying history will tell you that exact birth years can change depending on who is doing the writing. And was Pat really sure that my bio-mother was 18? She never told me how she knew her age. Maybe she read it, or did she just make it up? Could my bio-mother really have just been 15 years old? And if Pat knew it, would she really tell me this? Not my Pat.

From Bettyjean's tree, we actually knew a lot about these women: when they were born, married and had children. So Tanya really stood out. Single in 1960 and until 1966, she had two more children after marriage. Born near Little Rock, married near Little Rock, so it stood to reason that she lived in Little Rock in 1960. Ultimately, that is what I looked for: a single, 18-year-old, local female first cousin of Bettyjean's. And Tanya seemed close enough.

Regardless, what happened to her? Even Alicia, the Master of the Search, couldn't find her. I began to think that if people want to disappear from the world, they go to Arkansas. Sites like Intelius and Spokeo and Peoplesoft all had records, and they are gems, but they often provide outdated information and addresses from a long time ago. Not to mention that so many landlines have been replaced with untraceable cellphones. I can't remember the last time I dialed 4-1-1—probably when I was first looking for Kevin's number.

From command central on my trusty sofa with the dogs, and fueled by strong coffee, I drove forward, emailing Alicia quickly back and forth during one dedicated weekend.

I looked up at one point to see Kevin watching me pecking away at the computer. I hadn't even noticed him coming into the kitchen.

"You're getting really boring," he said with a smile.

"I know," I said, "But just let me roll with this. We're so close!" The search was quickly becoming addicting—and contagious! Before long, Kevin would find himself caught up in his own family search. But I did feel that Alicia and I were closing in on something important, and I just couldn't slow down. All my energy at that point went to finding out more about the most likely candidate to be my bio-mother: Tanya.

The search peaked! We knew Tanya married Calvin Wall in 1966, so probably—unless divorced—she had the last name *Wall*. Alicia went with that and finally found a retired Baptist preacher, Calvin Wall, living 90 miles from Little Rock. There were about seven addresses and as many phone numbers for him on the Internet. Determining the current address and phone number proved impossible. Let me say, though, I had no fear trying to Facebook or emailing people and simply explaining that I had done a DNA test and was now looking for family... *Are you interested in helping*? I would have to gauge the interest of the person. I did draw the line at calling a stranger out of the blue asking if she'd given up a baby in 1960. My style is strong, but not insensitive.

Fortunately, Alicia found a Calvin Michael Wall Jr. born in 1968. A half brother? Maybe. We found an email address for him and I fired off an immediate email asking for his help.

Hi Michael,

My name is Frank Billingsley and I'm a weatherman in Houston (this is to give you plenty of Google information so you know I'm not trying to award you a foreign lottery). I've been doing DNA testing because I am adopted, and have found a LOT of family. It looks like we are definitely cousins, maybe more! I am a cousin of Bettyjean, who you probably know. Are you at all interested in helping me with my search? If so, let me know and I will be happy to pay for it.

That would become my standard approach. I figured since I wanted his DNA results, I could at least fork over the 99 bucks. After all, if Michael Wall Jr. and I were half brothers, then I had found my biological mother. If a first cousin, then I would know to look at his aunts.

I had the first answer right away. The email bounced right back. Yet, Michael did have a Facebook account, although I knew sending a message would go into his "other" Facebook account since we weren't friends. I sent the message anyway and sent him a friend request. And waited.

While I waited, I tried to learn as much as I could. As it turned out, this research would provide the maps that charted the whole course, at least in terms of understanding how it all works.

Fish in all ponds, advised Richard Hill. Shortly after my February results came in, Morgan suggested I read Richard's book *Finding Family: My Search for Roots and the Secrets in My DNA.* His roller coaster ride started when Richard found out before college of his adoption. Through a slew of questions, letters, phone directories, innuendo, and the earliest of DNA testing, he eventually determined his biological mother, father, and siblings. His biological parents were deceased, but his half siblings were alive and well (some living right up the road from me in Houston!).

Thinking back on Brian Mixom and the article that launched me on this journey, I wondered again if I'd find anyone alive. My biological mother and father would be around 71 or 72, so it seemed likely. I had hope. Of course, "alive" is one thing. Wanting to see a long lost son is a whole other thing.

Shoving that fear aside, I wrote Richard an email and told him of my search. He quickly suggested getting my DNA to as many testing sites as available. FTDNA has hundreds of thousands of people who've tested their DNA. So do *Ancestry.com* and *23andMe.com.* I ordered them all. The more of my DNA out there to compare to, the more likely the puzzle pieces would fall into place. Richard knows whereof he speaks. He had spent four decades finding family. I felt almost embarrassed to be so far along in three months.

Another important piece of advice came from the Yahoo Adoption Search group. There are many such groups to aid in DNA adoption searches, and these folks are all pretty easy to find on the Internet, but they sometimes require that you sign up to become part of the group. They are experienced and knowledgeable and offer a wealth of free advice. Their advice to me stated directly: get your non-identifying adoption information. Pronto.

Back when my bio-mother carried me, social workers or "case workers" would interview women to gain as much information about the situation as possible and to offer motherly solace. What is interesting is that if you are adopted and obtain this information, you'll probably know much more about your own birth situation than most people know who are raised by their natural parents. The original documents contain the whole story, but adoptees will only get redacted or truncated portions. I have no idea exactly who decides what is permissible to pass on to an adoptee and what should still remain private, but usually, adoptees are given some or even all of the following:

- Birth mother's age at time of child's birth
- Her educational background
- Her religious affiliation
- Her physical description
- Her medical history
- Her family nationality
- Professions of the birth mother and her birth parents
- If the birth mother and father were single or married
- Her hobbies
- Why she put her child up for adoption

There's no guarantee I would get nearly that much. I really had no idea.

How many times had Pat told me, "Your mother was very pretty and smart, and your father played a lot of sports very well." But, come on, you're going to tell your adopted son that his biological parents started out stupid and ugly and sat on the bench?

And how many times had I come back with "What do you think I would be like if I was your real son?" only to be reassured.

"Not as good, honey. Not as good."

I couldn't have asked for a better answer to that question. Thinking about our little ritual of reassurance as I believed I was getting closer to finding these people I had wondered about for so long, I was thankful to Pat for her "parental upgrade" to smart and buff. But, as an adult, concern that the truth could be far from those happy stories began to pop up more frequently the closer I got.

After contacting Richard Hill and taking his advice to fish in all ponds, I dutifully read his book. I ordered additional DNA tests. I found the Arkansas Bureau of Vital Statistics website and printed out the forms for my non-identifying information, had a notary at work swear by me, picked up a five-dollar money order at the Quick-Mart, and sent it all off.

"They have 65 business days to get it to me, and it's been six." I told Alicia, who'd been reminding me to get that adoption information. The math meant it would arrive June 26th, almost three months away. I even called the very polite and helpful Charlotte Montgomery, who is in charge of the whole deal. She assured me in very polite terms there were many, many other people waiting for similar information. Stacks of requests, she said. I would just have to wait. Take a DNA test and wait. Send an email and wait. Send a DNA kit to someone else and wait. Ask for your adoption information: just wait.

In the meantime, Mark Brown's (adopted Hensley) Autosomal DNA search results—the search of all the DNA that we share, mother and father—results came back. I clicked open the email excitedly, only to discover we shared .4% of DNA: at best, a third cousin once removed. Not even close to a brother. I felt deflated. All this waiting and hoping, with nothing getting me truly closer to my bio-parents. And since neither Mark nor I had family trees on the Hensley side, it seemed unlikely we'd ever find out our common ancestor. We were Hensley cousins thanks to some great-great-someone or other and shared the Hensley name and nothing more.

I shut the computer and sat quietly in the kitchen. What was I doing? Was Kevin right? Was I getting boring with all this research, leading to nothing? There are so many people in the world, so many adopted people, and mind-boggling amounts of DNA. There were proverbs warning about this kind of search—needle in the haystack came to mind first. Then I felt a push against my leg, and a warm furry head appeared on my lap. It was one of our schnauzers, Ocean. His bright round eyes looked up at me, wondering why I was so uncharacteristically still. I laughed. Dogs! Dogs are all adopted, and they don't wonder about their biological parents. Maybe I should take the hint.

12

ADOPTION ON THE RADAR!

When I turned 10, Sharon and I relentlessly begged Pat and Jimmy for our own puppy. The *World Book Encyclopedia* had an entire dog section. I pored over the pictures of different pups and settled on cocker spaniels. Perhaps those sad eyes and big ears spoke to me, but I just had to have one. My parents went over the entire deal that all parents do: you will feed him, bathe him, walk him, take care of him, and do you promise that you will really do all of these things, because he is going to be *your* dog! Ha. Not hardly.

Smoky entered our life, finally, in 1972 and spent a wonderful twelve years as part of the Billingsley family. Somehow, my mother taught him to talk, which didn't surprise anybody, considering she majored in talking.

"Do you want a dog treat?" she'd baby talk to him.

"Woo-woo-woo," Smoky would wail. "Woo-woo-woo."

"Do you love Mommy?" More wooing. He would "talk" to me occasionally, but for Mom he performed every time and on cue. Although I would never have admitted it at the time, it was pretty cute.

So when I became an adult, I had to adopt my own dog. I got very lucky.

"I need a home for Rock Hudson, Frank," my friend Jerry said between sets at the gym.

"Huh?" I had no clue what he was talking about.

"A dog, Frank," he said. "I named him that because he's so handsome. I have his mother, and he was pick of the litter; but his personality is just too strong. His poor mom is withdrawing. I have to find him a loving TV weatherman."

"What kind of dog is he?" I asked, intrigued.

"Schnauzer. Silver."

I honestly didn't know much about schnauzers, but agreed to a meet and greet.

It took seconds and, like so many had with his namesake, I fell in love with Rock Hudson. In 1995, just before I met Kevin, I had firmed up my new contract as chief meteorologist at KPRC and had just bought a new house. It needed a dog to make it a home.

And Rock turned out to be the smartest of dogs. At just six months, completely house-broken, he would sit, shake, lay, play dead, and stay off the good furniture. He free-fed, meaning I would fill his bowl full and he'd just eat what he needed, rather than scarf every bit for the sake of it. So he never got fat. Honestly, the vet would bring people into her office just to show them the Remarkable Rock. I cuddled to sleep with him every night and would wake up in the morning with Rock at my feet.

In 2003 our management approached me wanting to adopt an official station weather dog. I had been arguing for the idea of a weather garden for at least some of our broadcasts. After all, what better place for the weatherman to be than *outside* in the weather? I'd seen such outdoor venues in other cities, and the idea in a place like Houston made perfect sense. At the time, those old HGTV shows, *Designer's Challenge* and *Landscaper's Challenge*, were popular, and that's exactly what I proposed: bring in three local landscape companies to pitch building us the perfect weather garden.

In return, whomever we picked would get the screen credit for the project, and I would get my outdoor weather studio.

Indeed, three different companies stepped up and presented an entire storyboard of their ideas and plans. AJ's Landscaping landed the deal, which thrilled me to no end, and we've enjoyed producing the 4 pm weathercast from that garden for better than 10 years now.

So what good is a weather garden without a weather dog?

After all, research had shown (and we research everything) that 52% of Houstonians lived with dogs—and there are scores of animal rescue groups and no-kill-shelters across southeast Texas. People, simply put, love their dogs like their family.

I had learned that the hard way in the beginning of my career. One frigid night I thoughtlessly remarked, "Bring your short-haired dogs indoors tonight, but if they have a good coat of hair, they will be fine." That was true—they would have been. But the dog owners poured down on me! "If you don't want to sleep out in that weather, neither does your dog—no matter what kind of hair they have!" I have never forgotten that lesson!

So in 2003, we began mulling over the idea of adopting a weather dog, not something that we rushed into. It was just like Pat and Jimmy's deal with me and Sharon: taking care of him, training him, figuring out how to really use him on television, and—most of all—finding the *right* dog were all considerations. We put our friends at the Houston Humane Society on alert that we were searching for the right pup (not too young, not too old).

In April 2004 the perfect Benjy-looking, happy-tailed dog arrived. Later, I spoke to his original owner, who literally adopted him out of a box in front of PetSmart and named him Fluffy (a moniker that described him perfectly). Unfortunately for this owner, someone reported her for having a dog at her apartment, and she had no choice but to give him up. We were grateful.

Fluffy loved popcorn (what dog doesn't), and we found out quickly that he would "work for food." This made him easy to train. We introduced the new weather dog one warm spring afternoon in, where else, the weather garden during the 4 pm news. We told viewers to go to our *Click2Houston. com* website and vote for their favorite name. Fluffy, we had decided, needed a more weather-appropriate TV name. Vote Now! Windy, Doppler,

Stormy, Rainy, or Radar. I took a liking to Radar, and luckily viewers agreed with me by a wide margin. The newly christened Radar became Houston's own beloved weather dog.

Just like humans have their own unique mix of DNA, so do dogs. In fact, as DNA science has expanded, there are services that will tell you exactly what the formula for your dog's mixed-breed is. We didn't do any testing on Radar, but by looking he seemed a Wheaton terrier, with other breeds mixed in his gene pool. He reminded me of Tiger from the Brady Bunch, and had quite a spoiled personality. We found groomers to groom him, trainers to train him, vets to vet him, and PR people who wanted him at *everything*. If Radar the Weather Dog appeared at an event, you can bet that people showed up.

For Christmas 2004, Foley's department store created a Radar dog doll—a perfect little fluffy stuffed animal. We announced that Radar and I would be at one of the stores in a local mall, and that Saturday morning we took pictures and signed autographs for hundreds of manic people who lined up to buy the Radar doll. Big demand. Radar had fans.

Management couldn't have been happier. I tried to adopt him as my third dog—I had gotten Hudson to accompany Rock. That immediately caused alpha dog issues in my home. The weekend Radar came over became a pee fest in the house, and, worse, on the master bed. Clearly, this particular combination of three dogs, all males, wouldn't work, so Radar never became "my dog" in the sense that I cared for him 24/7. He did, however, become the beloved dog of one of our producers.

For three years, Radar served faithfully as our on-air weather dog. He could wave at the camera to say hello or goodbye. He would sit or bark on command, stand up, and twirl around to dance. We even built a "Radar set" in the studio for him. Anchor Bill Balleza, who is a hobbyist woodworker, crafted a beautiful doghouse, complete with a flat roof, so Radar could sit up high for his camera shots. On command, he would step on a big red button, causing different forecasts to appear on the side of the set (hopefully that matched mine)! No longer just in the weather garden anymore, Radar had become so popular that he soon appeared in every weather segment. Even well-known dog lover Ellen DeGeneres played a video clip from one of our newscasts that showcased Radar the Weather Dog.

With such a following, you might wonder why Radar only lasted three years on TV.

In 2007, new management stepped in and began to diminish Radar's presence, until in 2008 they simply said, "We love him, but no more." The research on him proved nothing conclusive, and a case could be made either way that Radar helped or didn't help with the ratings. All about ratings, at the end of the day.

But I can make the case that he did make a difference. For instance, a woman wrote to me that her mother suffered from Alzheimer's, and Radar's daily appearance on the news truly lifted her spirits. *The only part of her day that brightens is when Radar shows up on TV.*

I knew we had to meet, so one afternoon I took Radar to the nursing home, where he sat with this special lady. I can't even begin to describe the smiles that broke out! She couldn't have been happier. And NASA celebrated one of its milestones down at Johnson Space Center and asked if they could make a spacesuit for Radar and invite me to bring him to the party. They did, and I did, and the employees will never forget Radar running around that room with his spacesuit on! Mission accomplished!

Radar's positive impact continued after his weather days were over. In November of 2014, Radar was diagnosed with paw cancer. Our station stepped up to bring attention to this deadly disease. Mast cell tumors are very common in dogs, especially those over ten years old, and early detection can be key to a successful treatment. But it's an affliction that really isn't well known, despite being so common. After a minor surgery to remove the growth, along with a preventive protein shot, Radar lived two more happy years. When he died in 2016, we had a pet-a-thon in his honor, and 100 dogs were adopted from the Houston Humane Society in a single day, 10 times the average rate of adoption.

I received countless emails and letters from people who adopted dogs because of Radar. Some of those people had lost a dog in the past, and the grief had been so deep that they thought they were better off never going through such a loss again. They had vowed to never adopt another dog—until Radar changed that sentiment for them. And really, the most important message we sent was this: if we, as a big TV station, could adopt a Humane Society rescue dog and show the world how much love and joy a dog brings into one's life, then maybe we'd help a few more dogs out there find homes. While many people know the importance of adopting a pet, seeing it on TV every day really brought the message home.

It goes back to the family formula. All families form with different combinations of the key ingredients. For me, family meant husband, child, and dogs, all together in this comfortable house. And adoption allowed that formula to add up to the happiness I was so grateful to experience. Adoptions can complete families—whether it's a single person adopting a cat or dog, a couple adopting their child, or a man like me in his mid-thirties finding a partner and helping to take on the responsibility of a young seven-year-old child.

Adoption and love happen on so many levels. Our dogs, Rock, Hudson, River and then Ocean have been integral parts of our family. I understand why people call their pets their four-legged kids. And now, with Ocean's bright eyes looking out at me from under his fuzzy white eyebrows, I knew that my pity party about Mark Brown's DNA results was over. I was too close to let this setback stop me.

13

COUSINS BY THE DOZEN

On April 5th, new DNA results from *23andMe.com* came back. Again, they included another thousand distant cousins to add to the Colonial Soup, although 12 close cousins were in the mix, generally listed as second to third cousins. At the very top, a woman popped up named Barbara Johnson with whom I shared 6% DNA.

100% = identical twins
50% = parent/child
50% = brother/sister
25% = half sibling
25% = grandparents/aunts/uncles
12% = first cousins/great-uncles/great-aunts/great-grandparents
6% = first cousins once removed
3% = second cousins
.5 to 1% = third cousins
Less than half a percent = distant cousins (4th, 5th, 6th etc.)

So now I had Barbara with 6%! That much DNA is unquestionably a first cousin once removed, even stronger than the match with Bettyjean's full 4%. *And* Barbara matched on my X chromosome, my mother's side! But where? Since *23andMe.com* uses a different chip analyzer than the other sites, I could not just upload Barbara's results to FTDNA to see how she compared to Bettyjean.

So I sent Barbara an email through *23andMe.com*, along the lines of my being adopted, looking for family, and her being my strongest match yet. *Do you have a family tree made, or could you tell me anything?*

Barbara answered within the day and shared what she knew. She had discovered late in her own life that the man who raised her was not her biological father. She had been fathered by a man named Larry Harmon, originally from Arkansas. Barbara's mother and Larry had had a long-term affair. Barbara had never known Larry, but she did get to meet him once before he died in the mid-1980s. She ended up with a lot of new cousins, most living in California. Apparently, the Harmon brothers had all left Arkansas after serving in World War II, seeking their fortunes in the Golden State. Barbara didn't fall on the Hensley Y side. Again, being an X-match meant we connected somehow through my mother's side, not my father's.

Bettyjean's tree had one lone Harmon born about 1900, who died sometime in the 1940s with no spouse or children that I could find. The 1940

Census, however, which I found on *Ancestry.com*, showed the Harmon family in Arkansas—a slew of boys and girls born anywhere from 1900 to 1924 to parents Walter and Naomi Harmon. I could trace them easily back to the mid-1800s, but any other census record on them stopped there, with nothing on Walter or Naomi's parents. Barbara did say that the name spelling had changed several times since the first Harmon had come over in the 1600s from Germany. So finding an extended tree would be difficult.

But now I had Barbara, a female first-cousin-once-removed, born in Bakersfield, California in 1954, related to me through my mother! It intrigued me that Barbara's biological history included what is called an NPE—a non-paternal event. In other words, the man she considered her father her entire life turned out not to be. Not really a Johnson, but a Harmon. Could my mother also be a Harmon? I had no idea. But I learned from the *23andMe.com* match that I needed to go fishing again.

Every strong match brought a new glimmer of hope—another path off the beaten trail. If a new clue meant forking over for another test, I didn't care. After my initial sinking spell when I hit a wall with Mark Brown, I was once again compelled by the mystery of the search. And there were happy endings. Barbara hadn't ever imagined that she had another father until the one she knew had died and her mother explained. And the family she discovered had been welcoming. Stories like this reassured me.

In late April, Michael Wall Jr., possibly a half brother, accepted my Facebook friend request. I explained that I thought we were cousins, given the Bettyjean connection.

Michael couldn't have been more willing and eager to test his DNA. In the late 1990s, when trying to put his own family tree together, he had actually posted on a web forum looking for relatives. He had no idea that Bettyjean had already done such thorough research. Although he knew who she was, his family had never been close to hers.

Our side of the family is all Church of Christ, hers is Mormon. We just didn't know them well, he explained. *But I can tell you, my mother isn't your mother and neither are any of her sisters.*

Had he talked to her? I didn't know, but I did know that just to get someone to agree to test their DNA is a huge help—I didn't have time for a lineage debate. Let the DNA chips fall where they may and tell the story.

I'll be glad to take the DNA test and help you in any way I can, he wrote.

If nothing more, Michael's test—if we shared the X—would definitely confirm that I was searching on the right path. Michael could only get his X from his mother, and that would, again, lead us back to great-grandmother Pearl, wife of Hank.

As April ended, I had the following:

- Bettyjean—first cousin once removed.
- Michael—either a half brother, a first cousin, or a second cousin. His DNA would confirm a lot!
- Barbara Johnson and the Harmons—first cousin once removed

I soon had a DNA kit from FTDNA on its way to Michael, and I had another DNA kit on order for me from *Ancestry.com.* I was fishing fast and furiously in all ponds.

"Another $99?" Kevin asked. "Lord!" My DNA testing had easily reached a thousand dollars. "We aren't really going to test everyone in America, are we?" He joked, but he had a point.

And Alicia made another frustrating point: *Are you sure it's through Pearl, Bettyjean's father's mother? Bettyjean's mother's side is still possible. You might be on the Mormon side, despite the logic. And that could be where the Harmon side came in.*

I just wanted answers! Somewhat reluctantly, I took a closer look at Gabe Baker, Bettyjean's grandfather on her mom's side. Researching all of his children and their children, I could rule them out as none of them had daughters, or the daughters were most likely too old or too young—probably. You never really know until you know.

Alicia offered two other important pieces of advice: *first, keep an open mind about teenagers: a thirteen year old is more likely to have put a child for adoption than an eighteen year old. Secondly, the non-id information is important and helpful, but can be full of inaccuracies.* That had never occurred to me—inaccuracies in my history from Pat?

One thing Pat and Jimmy shared was their practicality. As my search had unfolded, I had told them, "I'm related to a Billingsley!" They were not interested. In their mind, I already was a Billingsley. I decided that she wouldn't have gone out of her way to make up anything about my birth parents beyond their basic wonderfulness. Given that she wasn't there, she didn't have a lot to work with anyway.

But my birth mother and the social workers and attending nurses and doctors were all there. They all knew what happened, didn't they? So how could there be inaccuracies?

Alicia inspired me with Chris Schauble's story. A Los Angeles television reporter, Chris had hired Jay Rosenzweig, private investigator, to find his biological family. In six months, Jay had turned up Chris' mother and half sister. Another man, my age, found Chris' story encouraging and hired Jay as well. A few months later he celebrated his mother's 76th birthday in Germany with her. So a PI approach existed, but didn't guarantee success or speed. Through this hurry-up-and-wait, fish-in-all-ponds, endless— and sometimes emotional—research, we seemed to be inching closer to answers. But where would those answers really take me? And to what end?

That question, in a very real sense, came up at a small dinner party the first of May. My search, from the initial DNA inquiry in December, had now consumed me for half a year. I decided it was time to talk about it with friends. I really had not said much to anyone, except my sister Sharon and Kevin. He and I were at a dinner party at the mid-century home of two dear friends in Bellaire. They are quite the foodies, and over a delicious brisket and Brussels sprouts, aided by several glasses of wine, I just let the whole story spill out. I hadn't realized how much I needed to talk about it, or how consumed I had been. I have a way of talking about myself too much and try to be very cognizant when people seem to be tuning out. But this dinner group was glued the tale of my DNA search.

In the past when people had asked if I had ever looked for my biological parents, I just said, "No, I'm really not interested." And I had thought no one else would be interested, either. Wrong, and wrong! Everyone around the table that night wanted to know exactly how it would play out. I ran through the timeline of finding my relatives to date, and how the trail wound back to Pearl and Hank Garland, my great-grandparents. That same trail would wind down to a female first cousin of Bettyjean who would be my biological mother, but she was eluding me.

One our friends spoke up. "So, what are you wanting out of this?" he asked.

"I don't want anything." True. I didn't need a thing. No kidney issues, no debtor's prison.

"You misunderstand me," he said. "You're doing this for some reason, right? What is it? What's your goal?"

I thought a moment and realized how far this had all gone from being an interesting experiment for a TV story. What *did* I want? Somewhere in my DNA, there was a science piece, a piece that recognized causation. Every watch has a watchmaker. Every air mass leads to a certain type of weather. When I report, I always include this information for my viewers. *This is the air mass we are watching in the Pacific, and here's why.* Reflecting on my friend's question, I saw that, initially, I wasn't so much after the people as I was the story. I was curious. And curiosity demands answers. But the Encyclopedia Brown adventure had begun to fade when real names of real people with real lives and histories started showing up. That had changed the goal entirely.

"Closure," I answered finally. "I suppose I would like some closure. I never thought I could really find out where I came from or how I happened to show up on this planet, at least not without a lawyer and a court order of some kind. But between DNA and genealogy, it's really possible to just follow the breadcrumbs." I looked across the table at Kevin, thinking about all my $99 breadcrumbs and the hours I had spent following them. "See where they lead." If you know your family history, then you are the magician who knows the secret of the trick. If you don't, then you are the audience, left to wonder.

My friends wished me luck. "Let us know what happens." After all, what could they really say?

When we got home that night, I plopped on the sofa and checked email, just in case there was some news. My search was out of the closet now, and sharing it had helped me to see how much it had come to mean to me. The Facebook icon had a little number on it. Clicking it, I found a message from my friend Peter Hensley.

I had sent a message to three Facebook friends named "Hensley" as soon as the first Y-DNA results had come out. One went to Peter: *Peter...*

I am adopted...had my Y-DNA tested, which is father to son DNA...I am a HENSLEY...We are probably cousins somewhere on that tree! How about that?

Now, two months later, Peter replied: *My grandfather Hensley was adopted!*

And there you have DNA. I am biologically a "Hensley" while Peter Hensley is biologically *not* a "Hensley." I was getting used to hitting the wall in my search, and I shut the computer and went up to bed. The next morning, I would find myself tempted to actually hit a wall.

14

MICHAEL WALLOWING

Waiting for DNA results can seem interminable, even though it only takes about three weeks. And you have to remember that not everyone is as interested as you are in getting those tests sent in, analyzed and charted. It's like keeping in mind that your wedding is your wedding, not theirs—your family search isn't at the top of everyone's to-do list. Some people will let the kit sit around for a few weeks before actually even doing the test. Imagine.

And so it happened with Michael Wall Jr. I didn't want to push too hard, but I knew his kit had arrived in early May. By now, late May, four weeks later, it still hadn't been sent back to Houston for analyzing. Had he decided against testing? Had he spoken with his mother, who simply said don't do it?

How could I get him going? Maybe it's finally time to hit the wall, literally, I laughed to myself. But as Pat always said, "You catch more flies with honey," so I finally settled on sending an encouraging note, and much to my relief, he got to it—on the first of June. He explained: *Apologies…somehow the DNA kit rolled under the car seat and I just found it…I'll get it in the mail today, I promise.* Like your wedding, no one cares as much about your family search as you do.

But Michael's delay gave me time to focus on Barbara Johnson's line and try to figure out how she fit into my tree. Her results weren't back yet either, but her father, Larry, showed up in the 1940 census, listed as Louis (go figure). I can see how misspellings happen, but census workers must have been overworked and underpaid in those days! The result of the Harmon family in the census:

- W L Harmon 50
- Naomi Harmon 47
- Ted Harmon 18
- Mark Harmon 18
- Bonnie Harmon 16
- Larry Harmon 14
- Johnny Harmon 12
- Ray Harmon 4

So we had the older twin boys, Ted and Mark, daughter Bonnie, Larry, and two more sons. The DNA results showed Barbara as first cousin to my bio-mom, but something simply didn't add up. My bio-mother couldn't be first cousins with Bettyjean *and* with Barbara unless Bettyjean and Barbara were on the same tree. Everyone had to be related somehow and, so far, they weren't.

I still needed to find the daughters of the older kids—Ray and Johnny would have been too young to be a father and Larry could be ruled out being Barbara's dad. I turned to her, and she had more information.

"Bonnie I really know nothing about. Ted and Mark had children, but not until after World War II, after they returned from the service and moved to California. Their children were all born in the late 40s and early 50s."

That seemed to leave Bonnie Harmon, born in 1924 as a possible grandmother. Mother to my mother, born in 1942? I stared at all of these family trees like a comatose cat, willing them to tell me something, but no answers were coming.

June 26th, Thursday, finally arrived. No non-identifying information arrived. Nothing. I felt so disheartened; but before I called Arkansas Vital Statistics and begged, I would give them a couple of more days. Everyone is overtasked with more work and fewer workers these days. I imagined one lone lady sitting in the back of a dusty warehouse, thumbing through stacks of cold case files, hunting down microfilm, scrolling and squinting through birth records and documents, gleaning permissible information for an adoptee to know and redacting accordingly. When I had talked to the lady in charge a couple of months before, she sounded exasperated. She made it clear that my non-id info would *not* be there even one second early. I took her at her word.

The weekend of June 28th, Sharon and I went to Arkansas in celebration of Pat's 80th birthday. Pat stood front and center. The day is special every year, since she and I shared a June 22nd birthday. My mother had waited a week to celebrate her big milestone because a neighbor's grandson's wedding on Saturday the 22nd had stolen the show for that particular weekend. Small towns can only accommodate so much celebration in one day.

Sharon and I met in Houston and flew to Memphis the morning of the 28th, driving the hour down to Helena for the big soiree. Sharon's son and daughter drove over from Birmingham, where they were living. Twenty or so of my parents' friends celebrated at the Helena Country Club, and we had a lovely early dinner, champagne and cupcakes.

I found myself at odds with my emotions that weekend. There I celebrated with my wonderful "tried and true family" who had raised me, while my thoughts were consumed with finding an unknown biological family from where I'd originated. While I had mentioned finding a Billingsley connection in my tree, I hadn't shared the details of my search with Pat and Jimmy. They are not the emotionally jealous types and have never played a single guilt card like some parents do. Still, throughout the process, I was always conscious of not wanting to cause any hurt feelings. Until I had more concrete answers, sharing the play-by-play seemed a bit dramatic. For now, I decided, I would keep the unfolding details—and frustrations—of tracking my biological family tree to myself. And I'm glad I made that decision. I didn't know it then, but that weekend would be the last time I only had my family as my only family. The DNA dam had splintered.

Sunday morning my cellphone pinged with the *Ancestry.com* email: *Your DNA results are in!* I glanced at the site on the way to the Memphis airport to see an easy 500 Viking cousins, but also two very strong matches. Following up on these matches would prove to be the most challenging part of my search, but ultimately the most rewarding.

15

THE HUNT CONTINUES

Results from Family Tree DNA had given me a Hensley last name, Bettyjean, and Michael Wall. *23andMe.com* gave me Barbara. Now, the *Ancestry. com* results showed two strong relationships:

- John McNeill of St Louis: First to Second cousins
- Steven Hilton of Little Rock: Second to Third cousins

At the time, *Ancestry* didn't reveal just how much DNA we shared, like the other two companies. They just simply put the determined relationship out there with confidence: *first to third cousins, very strong confidence level.* The real plus about these new matches was that both of these men had family trees posted. It's always a nice advantage when someone has done a little homework for you! And Steven lived in Little Rock.

I easily followed Steven's tree. His maternal line went right to his mother, Floy, and from her to his grandmother, Elsie, and from her to his great-grandmother, Adele *Garland*.

Steven→Floy→Elsie→Adele Garland

I knew THAT last name! Hank and Pearl Garland were the grandparents of Bettyjean! A huge lead! Pearl definitely looked to be the "common ancestor" I had suspected! And it made perfect sense that Steven's great-grandmother, Adele Garland Jones, would be the sister of Hank Garland. And my being Hank Garland's great-grandson would put me exactly at third cousins with Steven, as *Ancestry.com* predicted. 99% confidence!

I wrote Steven a quick note:

Hi Steven,

I have had some new information come my way that I'd like to share. The bottom line is that Adele Garland, your great-grandmother, appears to have been my great-grandmother, also. I have done a lot of DNA testing of various people and I'd like to share it all with you if you are interested. And I would like very much to know more about Adele's descendants if you can help me.

Thanks
Frank Billingsley

Steven wrote me back:

I would love to help you. Adele was my great-grandmother. I met her once or twice when she was already very old. As I recall she was living with one of her granddaughters. Anyway, I don't have a lot of info on the Garlands but I DO have a bit on HER ancestry and I can give you some names of her descendants. I'm sorry I don't get on here as often as I should. I DO want to compare notes though. I reconnected with a sister through genealogy on my dad's side. And we are still in touch.

He helped more than he realized, by both encouraging me with his own success and inviting me to have a look at his full family tree. Adding Steven's information, *my* family tree now looked like this:

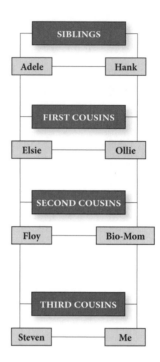

This information also clarified one important point: if Bettyjean's mother's side, her Mormon relatives, were my side, then I would *not* have been related to Steven Hilton this strongly. Finding out that he and I were third cousins, with ancestors going back to Pearl and Hank and Hank's sister, Adele, firmly put me on Bettyjean's father's side: the Garland side. At least I knew that all along I had been following the correct branch of the tree. And Bettyjean nailed it– she had always insisted that she'd have known anyone on the Mormon side. She knew I must be a Garland.

This simple third cousin relative sealed that deal, and I had *Ancestry. com* to thank for it. Fishing in all ponds was yielding a good catch. Pearl Jones Garland had to be the common ancestor to all these maternal relatives. Or so I thought at the time—I hadn't contacted John McNeill yet.

16

INTO AFRICA

ack in Houston after the big birthday party in June, I called the Arkansas Bureau of Vital Statistics first thing Monday morning. I took a deep breath and put on my best *please-help-me-as-you-promised-you-would* voice.

"Hi, Ms. Montgomery," I identified myself, and she seemed to mull over my name, vaguely remembering me like we were at a high school reunion.

"Oh, yes. I see you right here."

"And you see my request from last March, and you promised I would have the non-id info by June 26th. Or maybe you just meant you would send it by then, and I just haven't gotten it yet?" I like giving someone an opportunity to "fix" a situation. Polite always wins.

"I'll send it out Wednesday," She said matter-of-factly, as if that had always been the agreed upon timeframe. "I'm moving you to the top." You gotta love her style: *I dropped the ball, but don't despair... I am going to take that ball and put it right in your hot little hands.*

"Thank you. I'll look forward to it." I felt a kind of relief, for at least there seemed to be a light at the end of this long reel of microfiche.

We hung up and I turned to my newest, strongest *Ancestry.com* relative, John McNeill. I started my email relationship with John pretty much like all the others:

Hi John, I am adopted, born 1960 in Little Rock. You are my highest match on Ancestry.com. I have also tested on FTDNA and 23andMe. com. I know through Y-DNA I am a "Hensley" and through my X matches I am Garland and Harmon on my maternal side. So I have no idea how we are related, but it looks like we are cousins! Frank Billingsley

John got back to me the same day:

Hi Frank, You are the highest match I have ever had, as well. I do not have any Hensley, Garland, or Harmon surnames in my tree. Is there any other info you can give me? Would you like access to my tree? I will add you as a guest. Regards, John McNeill

What was *this*? John comes in as one of my strongest matches yet and has not a *single* name from my other searches on his tree? Hensley would be my father's side, Garland my mother's side, Harmon "somewhere" on my mother's side. There aren't any more sides—just the two. He had to be on one of them! And, a quick check of Bettyjean's tree revealed no McNeills, not a one.

And, of course, I looked a lot like John, whose picture had bright blue eyes like my own, despite his being a couple of decades older than me. To be honest, since my search had started, I thought *everyone* looked like me. It's just how it goes—we strain to see a resemblance in the hope that this will substantiate a relationship. Usually, nothing could be further from the truth. I Googled him and discovered that he lived in St. Louis and ran a hunting tour-guide business. He sponsored groups that photographed the wild game in Canada and Africa, and his website boasted incredible pictures from these trips.

"The Journey of a Lifetime" his website proclaims proudly. "Come home to Africa." I couldn't help but recognize that in terms of *Ancestry.com*, we *all* started in Africa 12,000 years ago and migrated from there. Every human being's lineage goes back to Africa. Come home, indeed!

Coincidentally, my adoptive maternal grandfather had taken to safari travel as well. The politically incorrect kind. Grandaddy had always been a big fisherman and hunter and, as such, went on safaris to help thin out overpopulated animal herds in Canada and Africa. And so his big house in Helena had filled up with these large animal trophies (a nice word for heads). Zebra and lion rugs rested on the floors, while elk, moose, and buffalo hung on the walls, mostly upstairs in the hallway and bedrooms. From their elevated perch they would stare menacingly at my sister and me when we visited. Try going to sleep in an old stone mansion while the dead eyes of a two-ton bison glare at you from twenty feet!

That last week of June turned out to be a big one for DNA results. Barbara Johnson, Michael Wall, Bettyjean, and Steve Hilton all firmed up many details on my mother's side; but John McNeill, first cousin, had no one matching with me anywhere. His tree and my tree had lots of names, but not a single one the same.

Finally, on Monday, July 7th, after four months of waiting, my non-identifying adoption information arrived.

17

SINGLE, SMART, & SAD

"It's here," Kevin whispered over the phone.

July 7, 2014. Kevin works from home, and I had been calling him from my office every afternoon, right about the time the mail would come. "Anything yet?" I'd ask impatiently.

Now it was here.

"Well, open it!" I said.

"I already have," said Kevin.

"Read it to me!" I said.

"No," said Kevin. "I want you to read it yourself."

For a split second, I considered another impatient retort. But he was right, and I appreciated his insight. So much I had been seeking for so long was in that document. I was going on the air in 10 minutes. I could barely concentrate on the forecast, my mind was so caught up in what that letter might reveal about my history.

Finally, when I came home for dinner I saw it. On the counter sat a regular-sized white envelope, certified, with my full name on the front and the return address from the Arkansas Department of Human Services. It looked just like any other business letter. Inside were *four* single-spaced typed pages of information that would change my life.

106

Division of Children and Family Services
Adoptions Support Unit

P.O. Box 1437 ·Little Rock, AR 72203
(501) 682-8462· Fax: (501) 682-8094 · TDD: 501-682-1442

July 2, 2014

CERTIFIED MAIL ARTICLE# 70051820000220191257

Frank Billingsley

Dear Mr. Billingsley:

I am providing you with the following information in response to your request for non-identifying information regarding yourself. You requested this information by forwarding a completed affidavit to the Arkansas Mutual Consent Voluntary Adoption Registry, which is administered by this agency. You explained the information you wanted is general background information along with any medical information that may be in your file.

The sealed record regarding your adoption is on file with this agency. It is on microfilm and has been reviewed. The following information is documented in your record.

You were born in a hospital on June 22, 1960. You weighed 7 pounds and 12 ounces and were 21 inches in length. Your head circumference was 36 centimeters and your chest measurement was 33 centimeters. Your weight at discharge from the hospital was 7 pounds and 8 ounces.

When you were six days old, your birth mother entered an Entry of Appearance, Waiver of Summons and Consent to the Appointment of a Guardian with Authority to Consent to Adoption without the Consent by Natural parent or Parents relinquishing you into the custody of the state for the purpose of adoption. You remained in foster care until you were legally adopted when you were six months old.

When you were six weeks old, you were examined by a doctor. You weighed 11 pounds. When you were eight weeks old, you weighed 12 pounds and 12 ounces. When you were three months old, you weighed 19 pounds and 4 ounces.

When you were four months old, you were placed in the home of your adoptive parents.

When you were five months old, your adoptive mother went to the worker's office to give an update on your progress in their home. Your adoptive mother did not bring you along for the visit due to the bad weather conditions. Your adoptive mother told the worker that you had gained two pounds since you were placed with them. You ate Pablum, fruit, vegetables and meat. You only took three bottle of milk per day. You slept through most of the night for the most part and were in fine physical condition. Your adoptive mother felt that they had no real adjustment problems with you; everything went smoothly.

At this time in your development, your shots were current. Your doctor told your adoptive parents that you needed to be circumcised, but wanted to wait until you were a little older. Your doctor suggested that they do it when you were about one year old. You were taking multiple vitamins and were on the formula Similac.

Your adoptive mother told the worker that she was pleased that you were born on her birthday.

During your birth mother's pregnancy with you she resided at a home for unwed mothers. During her stay, she was interviewed by a worker for the agency. It is documented in your file that your birth mother had been referred to the agency by a doctor from her hometown. Your birthmother told the worker that her mother was deceased and she resided with her maternal grandmother. She also stated that her grandmother received public assistance for her until she graduated high school.

Your birth mother was nineteen years old at the time of your birth. The worker documented that your birth mother was a pretty girl with nice features. She had a small bone structure. She was 5 feet and 5 inches tall and weighed 118 pounds. She was extremely nervous. This was evidenced by her quick chatter, her motions and the fact that her nails were bitten down to the quick and by her admission that she had always been quite nervous. The worker documented that your birthmother had a rather odd facial expression- not much animation and her face had a white pallor and her eyes had a starring quality about them.

Your birth mother had a younger brother, age 16, and a sister, age 14. Each of the three children had a different father. Your birth mother had always lived with her maternal grandmother. Her grandmother told her that her mother was not married to her father, although she carried his name. Your birth mother stated that she did not remember her father, but that he came to see her when she was small. She met her father's brother when she was older. He told her that her father owned a supermarket in another state.

Your birthmother's mother died when her sister was born. Your birth mother was five years old at the time of her mother's death. Your birthmother's grandmother was seventy-four years old at the time of your birth. She had heart trouble and high blood pressure. She received Old Age Assistance. Your birth mother had a maternal uncle. He was a bachelor and helped out with finances. He did "day-work" on farms.

Your birth mother told the worker that she had a kidney infection during the first trimester of her pregnancy with you. She also had an infection of the cervix. She had never had any illnesses. She had shingles twice during the year prior two your birth, each incident was a month apart. She commented to the worker "that's a nervous condition, isn't it?" When asked why she thought this, she stated that it was because her "kin folks" were always down on her because she was born out of wedlock. They would say to her that she was the ruin of the family and call her names. One thing that they would call her is "bastard". Her grandmother on the other hand, was extremely protective of your birth mother. She did a lot to make your birth mother dependent on her.

In school, your birthmother made good grades. Her relatives resented this because their children did not make good grades. When asked if she had anyone outside of her grandmother with whom she was close to when growing up, she said she had a teacher that she liked whom she would take her problems to. Other than this teacher, she had no one else.

Your birth mother discussed her plans for you with the worker. According to the worker, she showed little effect in discussing you. She said she was not sure as to what she wanted to do, but that she would probably place you for adoption because she could not afford to take care of a baby.

Your alleged birth father was twenty-two years old at the time of your birth. He was 5 feet and 11 inches tall and weighed approximately 170 pounds. He had brown hair and brown eyes. Your birthmother believed that he was a high school graduate. He was a truck driver. He was not married.

Your birth mother and alleged birth father dated for about six months. She told him about her pregnancy with you. She said that it made her mad when he did not believe her. As a result, she went back to her hometown. Four months later, when she came back and she told him about her pregnancy with you again, after she had seen a doctor, he still did not believe her. Your birth mother admitted that they only used contraceptives "sometimes". Your birth mother was very upset over his attitude and did not know what to do. She stated that she would have liked to marry him, if he were willing to marry her.

While your birthmother resided at the home for unwed mothers, she could not relate to the other girls in the home and group living. After talking with your birth mother, the worker decided that your birth mother would get along better in a foster home setting. As a result, she was later moved to a foster home. She got along well with the foster mother, but got into a lot of arguments with the girls in the home. She played canasta with the foster mother and other girls. She was rather lazy doing chores around the home and the other girls complained about her not doing her jobs.

Before your birthmother gave birth to you, her mother's sister, wrote her about you, which upset her. She and her husband drove to the foster home and asked to see your birth mother. Your birth mother did not want to see them. Her foster mother told them that visiting was not allowed in the foster homes. Your birth mother's aunt called the Governor's office about this. The Governor's Office then called the worker and asked the worker to speak with your birth mother's aunt. In the meantime, the worker learned from your birth mother that her aunt was a sick woman and had been in the State Hospital. When the worker contacted your birth mother's aunt, her aunt was very hostile at first. She demanded that the worker allow her to see your birth mother. The worker told her that she could not and that your birthmother did not want to see her. Your birth mother's aunt told the worker that she did not understand as she had always loved your birth mother. She went on to say that she was ill and would probably not live past a month. She added that she just wanted to know if your birth mother was alright. The worker assured her that your birth mother was fine.

Later, the Governor's Office called the worker again. Your birth mother's aunt called the worker again and the worker went through the conversation as she did previously. Your birth mother's aunt asked the worked if she would call her when your birth mother delivered you. The worker told her that it would be up to your birth mother to let her know if she wanted to at the time she would be in the hospital. In discussing it with your birth mother, she told the worker that she would rather that her haunt not be at the hospital when she delivered.

On the date of your delivery, your birth mother had nerves just before she went to the hospital. The doctor talked with her, but did not give her tranquilizers. After you were born, your birth mother went back to the foster home until she was able to travel. She wanted to go back to her grandmother's a while before looking for a job.

Seven days after your delivery, your birth mother went to the worker's office to sign the consents to release you for adoption. The worker documented that she did not cry in the office, but did on the way back to the foster home.

One week later, she returned home on a bus.

This is all the genetic, social, health and medical history contained in your sealed record regarding you, your birth mother, her family, your birth father and his family. I hope this information is helpful to you. If you have any questions, you may reach me at 501-682-8462.

Sincerely,

Adoption Services Unit

I am not sure, in retrospect, what exactly I expected this non-id info to really say. I guess I thought I'd get one page, like a press release, stating my birth mother's religion, education, health stats, and a quick explanation of why she chose adoption. Instead, I found myself reading the drama of a young girl full of nerves, a bit lost, and left to her own devices in a strange town.

I sat in shock, my eyes welling up. My 19-year-old single birth mother, a poor-as-a-possum farm girl, abandoned by her own father before even being born, losing her mother when only a small child herself. Then while still growing up herself, she wanted to marry my truck-driving birth father, who didn't even believe her pregnancy story and drove his truck away as fast and far away as he could. I felt horrified. And so sad. Everyone in her life seemed to leave her. Including me.

The story brought home my own fate, as I too came into the world with no promises. Life turned out pretty well for me, but undeservedly. I did nothing to change my fortune; it somehow changed for me. In that instant, I realized this had become so much more than just science at work. I felt that same feeling you have when an 18-wheeler almost creams you in a snow storm on the freeway: a call so close you literally stop the car on the side of the road and start crying and thanking God. My heart tore between the disparate realities of being born an impoverished orphan, from a family who had absolutely nothing, only to be blessed with a fortunate turn some higher power brought to my life. My stomach hurt with pain for my biological mother, called a "bastard" by her own family, shunned for her smarts and just trying to make a better go of it all. Suddenly, she finds herself pregnant, poor, and alone. And yet, once I'm born, she is not simply relieved or happy that this burden is now gone, but rather she cries as she leaves me behind.

I had to find her, now more than ever.

18

SEND IN THE A TEAM

*H*i *Frank,*

This is a fascinating case. You share too much DNA with too many people for this not to make sense. Angie is brilliant and will help you solve this one. Let me know what happens!

CeCe

Morgan Hawthorne's good friend and colleague, CeCe Moore, is a name a lot of genealogical gurus will recognize. "Your Genetic Genealogist," CeCe organized the first Finland Genealogical conference and is a full time genetic genealogy consultant for television shows like "Finding Your Roots" and Facebook's DNA Detectives. When I contacted her, she was consumed with organizing and running the 2014 International Genetic Genealogy conference in Washington, DC, but she kindly recommended her colleague, Angie Bush, to help with my case.

Angie lives in Salt Lake City, home of the great genealogical library. She boasts degrees in molecular biology and biotechnology and worked in the biotech industry for several years before creating her own career as a genetic genealogist. When we met, she was trying to get her own consulting business off the ground, and would spend time helping CeCe with cases she became aware of. Currently, Angie is on the board of directors for the National Genealogical Society, and is a senior genealogist researcher with Ancestry ProGenealogists in Salt Lake City. Angie is one of those researchers who is able to see the whole picture of just how this magical DNA can combine and recombine to produce us human beings.

I have played a lot of competitive bridge in my life and have always marveled at those savants who can look at their own bridge hand of 13 cards and, just by hearing a few bids at the table, can pretty well tell you exactly where all the other 39 cards are. Truly, there are people who can do that. Angie is to genealogy what bridge master Charles Goren had been to the bridge table. Sorting out difficult relationships is her specialty. She finds the cards. Morgan and I agreed we needed an objective eye on all of this. There were just too many relationships that didn't make sense. But we did have a tree, which had blossomed with the non-identifying information:

- My great-grandmother: 74 years old in 1960, therefore born in 1886.
- My grandmother: died in childbirth in 1945. Born when?
- My grandfather: owned a supermarket in another state. Had at least one brother, if not more.
- My mother: 19 years old in 1960; born in 1941
- My mother's brother: 16 in 1960; born in 1944
- My mother's sister: 14 in 1960; born in 1946
- My father: 22 in 1960; born in 1938. Truck driver, local or long-distance?

These were all people on my family tree, many with birth years, and they were all related one way or another to each other. In addition, we knew some DNA relationships that existed on my birth mother's side:

- Bettyjean: first cousin once removed or a second cousin
- Michael Wall: second cousin or second cousin once removed
- Barbara Johnson: first cousin once removed (her mother and my bio-mother *must* be first cousins)
- Steven Hilton: third cousin

And we had Pearl as a common link:

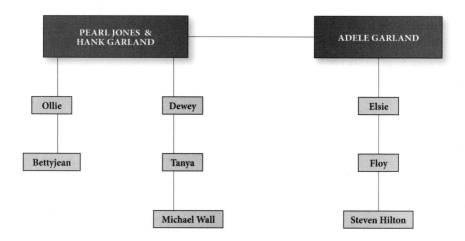

Pearl Jones Garland presented a minor problem: her birth year was listed as 1882, not 1886. I needed her to be born in 1886, so she'd be 74 years old in 1960. Saying that, anyone who has looked through the Find-A-Grave website, studied death certificates or pored over census records will tell you that as frequently as these documents are right, they can certainly be wrong. And the non-id information had not been truly verified. This story told whatever my biological mother said to the social worker during her interview, or perhaps even in a series of interviews. Did my biological mother really know her grandmother's precise age? Did her grandmother know her own correct age? Did anyone care about birth years until Social

Security created the need in 1935? And how many people knock a couple of years off, for good measure?

I felt overwhelmed. I had been through so many anticipatory moments at this point that I became emotionally exhausted. The information seemed so close, and yet it was still so far away from any concrete names. I had to just shake my head and push the cards into the center of the poker table: No fold, simply *all in*. I had done everything I knew to do. With all the DNA tests we had run, along with the new non-id info, surely Angie could sort it out. If Bettyjean's tree had my biological mother on it, then putting the new info into the hands of an expert of this caliber should lead us to her. And Alicia would be able to help. Her search techniques would put any private eye to shame, and she needed only a hint to figure out connections. Angie and Alicia: I called them the "A team."

And I would soon discover a third member of this team: Aunt Janie. What a sweetheart she would turn out to be!

19

DOUBLE OR NOTHIN'

I think I owe Angie Bush a new pair of glasses. As she delved into all of the DNA matches and non-identifying information, she realized that the connections simply didn't make sense. We knew Bettyjean and Michael Wall were related—Bettyjean and his mother were first cousins. And they both were direct descendants of Pearl Garland. They were first or second cousins to me on my mother's side, so my mother had to be on their tree. However, Barbara Johnson, also on my mother's side, showed up as a stronger first cousin match to me than both of them put together. And Bettyjean's tree had her nowhere! It was somewhat comforting to realize that this stumped the expert, too.

Then Angie texted: *Call me!*

"Hi!" I said when she answered. "What's going on?"

"Well," she explained. "I've been up all night trying to figure this thing out. You share enough DNA with Bettyjean to be a first cousin once removed, but not really as much as I think you should." She explained high and low DNA limits and how one daughter can look so much like Grandma and the other doesn't. Recombination can go a lot of ways! There is a range in all relationships and sometimes people have more. "It's like you're almost there at about 4%, but not quite. So it looks to me like a perfect case of double-dipping."

"Double what?"

"Double-dipping, or double cousins. In other words, I wondered if Bettyjean's grandmother and grandfather might have been fully related to your great-grandmother and great-grandfather."

"Okay, this is sounding illegal," I laughed, a little confused.

"Oh, not at all! It happened a lot then and still happens now. In other words, this is a case of you-marry-my-brother and I'll marry yours," Angie explained.

The key proved to be Steven Hilton, just a third cousin, but one whose tree pointed to Adele Garland, Hank Garland's sister. Steven's tree, however, didn't offer anything more than that—nothing on Adele's husband. *Who was Adele's husband?*

"What if," Angie thought, "Adele married Pearl's brother and Pearl married Adele's brother?" These intermarriages, as they are called, happen a lot, and especially did a hundred years ago when the closest neighbors might be the next farm down. At first glance it looks like a family cousin marriage, but it's not. It's simply one brother and one sister marrying the brother and sister of another family.

And *that* is exactly what happened. Adele Garland married Joe Jones and Pearl Jones married Hank Garland. Consequently, I shared *double* the amount of DNA with Bettyjean as one would normally assume. And double the amount with Michael Wall. Rather than the almost 4% throwing me and Bettyjean into first cousin once removed territory, we really should be considering half of that—around 1.5 to 2%. We were second cousins or second cousins once removed. And Michael Wall really shared just enough to be a third cousin. The situation was quite different than it first appeared. We were related, but not nearly as strongly as I first believed. The DNA didn't lie, but being doubled up, it made the relationships appear much stronger than they really are.

So now I had an explanation as to why we had such a huge DNA share. But where did it lead? How did I relate to all these people? Adele, Pearl, Joe, Hank were all brothers and sisters marrying each other, and all with an ark full of kids… kids who had more kids, like Bettyjean, Michael, and Steven.

Then Angie had more news. "I went to Find-A-Grave and found Adele's gravestone, Frank. Born in 1886! Exactly the year that would make her 74 years old in 1960!"

The non-id info had said that: "*Your birthmother's grandmother was seventy-four years old at the time of your birth.*" Adele had to be my grandmother, the one my biological mother lived with her whole life!

Adele Garland Jones: 1886—1983

I had found my great-grandmother. Not Pearl, but Pearl's sister-in-law! I finally had a name! Adele Jones! And she sure lived a long time, which offered a little comfort. So now my mission turned to finding her daughter, who would be my grandmother, and her daughter, who would be my bio-mother. Simple.

Hardly.

20

DYSLEXIC GRAVESTONES

Give Alicia Hall a name and she takes it from there. I sent her a quick email Saturday evening explaining Angie's find and the whole "double cousin" relationship. More importantly, I filled her in that Adele, not Pearl, had to be the connection to my bio-mother.

Then, for good measure, I texted Alicia, too: *Adele, 74 years old in 1960, my great-grandmother. She and her husband, Joe, must have had children, and one of their daughters would be my grandmother who would be my mother's mother.*

She texted back: *Time to pull out those census records!* I remembered that they stopped at 1940 and the 1950 census wouldn't be released until the year 2020. Alicia continued: *Your mother's birth in 1941, along with the half-aunt and half-uncle means she will not show up in any census. I'll have to find Grandma Jones!*

Alicia is one of those true night owls—often up until three in the morning. She went to work on this whole thing that Saturday night.

Alicia texted: *They had a ton of kids. This won't be easy.*

Adele Garland Jones and her husband, Joseph, indeed took the biblical instructions seriously: Be fruitful and multiply. Their nine kids consisted of five boys and three girls. Forget the boys; the girls were the candidates to be my grandmother:

- Elsie, b. 1903
- Flossie, b. 1911
- Marie, b. 1923

I gave her my quick assessment: *Elsie can't be her because she's Steven Hilton's grandmother. But at least we're in the right group of daughters!*

Alicia agreed: *And Flossie seems too old at age 30 to be giving birth to your mother and then left by a man.*

Alicia ruled out Marie within the hour, finding a gravestone stating she died in 1966:

Your grandmother died in 1945, so that's not her.

I texted right back: *She must be the crazy aunt calling the Governor. Now what? Alicia, that's it, that leaves no one else to be my grandmother and without her, no mother.*

Alicia: *Not giving up yet. People get left out of the census all the time.*

The census, first and foremost, determines population by state to determine representation in the House of Representatives. That is the primary reason it started, although clearly a lot more information is gleaned from the census, then and now. But counting bodies is the goal, and the actual spelling of names and exact birth year of those bodies came second. Let's face it: there are lots of people to count in a short amount of time. Precision when going door-to-door with a pencil and paper just didn't always happen.

With her experience, Alicia knew better than to just stick to the census.

She texted me optimistically: *I need to shake some family trees. If they're not in one tree, they're in another.*

The reasoning is simple. If the people you are finding don't fit what you know, then maybe not all the people are there. Look in another tree. Look in another census. Look in a different genealogical collection. Whatever you do, just keep looking! Find a name!

I had just gotten home around midnight when my cellphone buzzed: *I found another daughter!* Alicia texted: *Bettyjean's tree somehow left her off!*

Unbelievable! Thirteen thousand five hundred names on the family tree that Bettyjean had sent me, yet the one single name I needed had somehow been left off the tree. It's one thing for the state of Arkansas to intentionally chop down my tree, but quite another to find that the most complete genealogical record in the world had it so close and yet incomplete.

I found her on another person's tree! Alicia's text exclaimed. *Right there on an Ancestry.com tree. Louisa Jones!*

And while census workers are in a hurry and name spellings can go awry, you'd think a cemetery would get it right. Alicia sent me a picture of Louisa Jones' small, rectangular gravestone from the Opika Cemetery in Arkansas. There were only three problems with it:

- First, it misspelled her name Louisa, *Lou-s-i-a*
- Second, it had her birth year as 1928
- Third, it had her death year as 1945, not 1946

How could a gravestone be so far off? If you have seen the names of the 1800s and early 1900s, you know that Louisa is a pretty common one. And 1928 would put Louisa's age at 13 when giving birth to my mother in 1941… meaning a conception at age 12? From the non-id adoption information, she died in 1946 during childbirth with my mother's sister "by another man." In fact, according to the non-id, Louisa had all three of her children by three different men, none of whom she married: my mother born in 1941, a son in 1944, and a daughter in 1946.

I texted Alicia: *Wow! This thing is really off, those gravestone makers didn't much care.*

I keep telling you, gravestones, census records, first-hand reports, they can all be wrong! Alicia had warned me a while back about non-id adoption information too: don't always believe its accuracy. But the information told such an explicit story, I found it hard not to believe it.

Exactly which part of it is not to be believed? I asked her.

All of it, Alicia told me. *Until it's been verified as true, don't believe any of it.*

So Alicia went with the properly spelled *Louisa,* who had never married any of the men with whom she had children. She also decided Louisa just might have been married to one of them and began to research marriage registries. After all, if Louisa had three different children by three different men, perhaps she at least applied for a marriage license, even if the ceremony never took place.

I found it! I found it! She did get married! Alicia's text woke me at two in the morning.

Familysearch.org, the free site from The Church of Jesus Christ Latter-day Saints is often full of information not found anywhere else. Alicia found the marriage license, obtained on December 11, 1943, and the marriage certificate. Louisa married Lawrence Thompson the next day, December 12, 1943. And on this marriage license, her age is given as 20 years old. This was yet another age, and it put her birth year at 1923 (the same as her sister?) instead of 1928 (the gravestone). Not that it mattered anymore, and not that anyone would ever verify it one way or the other, but it serves as one of those frustrating examples that makes me admire people who commit themselves to years of genealogical research.

I found it to be an interesting coincidence that Louisa chose the date 12/12 to marry, just as Kevin and I had! The date fell on a Sunday back in 1943, while our 12/12 was a Wednesday in 2012. We had the same date, and neither occurred on a more typical Friday or Saturday which most people pick for a wedding. I wondered if Louisa and Lawrence married on a weekend because he had to get back to service duty on Monday morning…such weekend weddings happened a lot during World War II.

My adoption information became suspect. Louisa *did* marry and she married a man named Lawrence. She married in 1943 and gave birth to her son in 1944. Most likely, Lawrence fathered her second daughter, born in 1946, although possibly a third father did exist.

We started looking for divorce papers and another marriage license, but, suddenly, the life-trail of Louisa came to a screeching halt. Certainly her birth had been sometime in the 1920s. She had her first child, my biological mother, in 1941 by an unknown man. We had her marriage record in 1943, and from the non-id she gave birth to my uncle in 1944 and my aunt in 1946, although her gravestone had her death date as 1945. I had to be honest with myself—we "knew" all of this, believing the same gravestone that had Louisa's birth year off by four or five years and misspelled her name. I felt a lot of quicksand surrounding this one.

And Alicia could find no death certificate and nothing else anywhere on Louisa. We had nothing more. We couldn't find an obituary, which might list my mother's name as one of her survivors.

I found Adele's obituary, but that had only her name and her husband's name, and those names I already knew. Other than leaving behind "many children, grandchildren, and great-grandchildren," the obit revealed nothing.

However, we did have one new, very important name from the marriage license: Lawrence Thompson. Just as Bettyjean had led to her grandmother Pearl, who had led to her brother Hank, who had led to my great-grandmother Adele, and now to my grandmother Louisa, we now had her one known husband, Lawrence: my step-grandfather, stepfather to my mother, and perhaps the father to my uncle and/or aunt. The search resumed!

The marriage license listed Lawrence's age right there with 20-year-old Louisa. He married at 22, and after Louisa's death perhaps he lived a nice long life—we were hoping for an Internet trail. If he were alive in 2014, it would make him 94.

Alicia wasted no time: *Got him!*

Lawrence Thompson: born in 1921, died in 2006. And she found his obituary:

Lawrence Thompson of St. Charles, Missouri—Lawrence Thompson, 83, died May 21, 2006. He was a tool and die maker.

Survivors include his wife, Janet, three sons, Lawrence, Mark, and Douglas Thompson; three daughters, Janie Warrington, Linda Hudson, and Leslie Prince; a sister, Belinda Groton of Memphis; 19 grandchildren, 25 great-grandchildren and a host of nieces and nephews.

Two names stood out on the list of survivors: son, Lawrence Thompson Jr., who must be my uncle born in 1944, and his daughter, Janie Warrington.

Presuming the survivors were listed oldest to youngest—Janie would be his first-born daughter, likely my half-aunt; if, in fact, this proved to be the same Lawrence Thompson.

Alicia's last text of the night popped up at 4 am: *Janie Warrington is in Boston, we'll look for her tomorrow. She must be your aunt and she will know your mother.*

"Of course, she will know my mother," I thought. "I am the one she'll have no clue about."

21

TEXTING FOR TREASURE

As I woke up that Sunday morning, my presumed family tree, at least on my mother's side, looked like this:

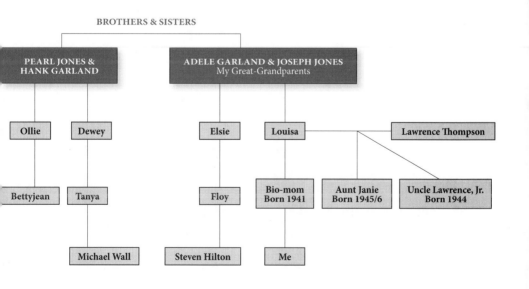

Bettyjean and my bio-mom were second cousins, not first. Michael Wall and I placed as third cousins. The double DNA share had fooled us all at first. Now I had every reason to believe I had found my half-aunt: Janie, born in 1946. No other clues could be found anywhere as to whom my bio-mom might be—Grandma Louisa had no obituary, and Great-grandma Adele's obituary listed no names.

Thank goodness, realtors put themselves all over social media hoping for a phone call. They live for contacts out of the blue. Their websites, email addresses, cellphone numbers all display on-line for the taking. But on that Sunday morning, July 13th, after two hours of scouring the virtual world, I located a Janie Warrington in Palm Springs, not in Boston. Maybe she had relocated there? She would be 67 years old now. A Palm Springs retirement might be nice, especially from the Polar Vortex of Boston. Bright blue eyes and a big smile lit up her Facebook page and helped convince me to just text her.

Hi Janie....this is your strangest text ever! I am a grandson of Louisa Jones, and I was born in Little Rock in 1960. I believe you are my aunt and know my biological mother. I can email you the whole story of how I figured this out or we can chat. I am a TV weatherman in Houston and you can easily Google me. We look alike, by the way! Oh and please don't freak out... I don't need an organ or anything! ☺ *Frank Billingsley*

I pressed the send button.

I poured coffee and stood by.

And by.

And by.

Nothing.

Except Kevin. "You're *texting* someone you don't even know, telling her that you are her long-lost-put-up-for-adoption nephew? Are you kidding me?" He just shook his head not knowing whether to admire my chutzpah or criticize my tactics. But I knew that he of all people understood my frustration of fishing with so many different poles. It was time to stop messing around and throw some nets.

Thirty minutes—a *ding* and a text back:

Wow, how did you get my phone number? I would love to chat about this. Not freaking, just curious...how did you find me?

"Oh, my God!" I exclaimed to Kevin. "She got my text! She's texting me back! I think it's her!" My fingers were shaking, typing out the next text: *I have been working with genealogists and friends and doing DNA tests. Your number was easy to find since you sell real estate, to be honest. This is very exciting! If my biological mother is alive please tell her I am looking for her so I can thank her.*

She replied innocently and with almost a confirmation, but still not enough to guarantee I had the right match: *That might be my half sister, Susan. She is very alive and I would love to talk about this. I am heading out to lunch right now, but more later! Can you call me this evening?*

Lunch? Really, I thought? I just shook my head and prepared for a conversation that would change my life.

22

BABY STEPS

———————

A secret. Of course. Why wouldn't I be a secret?
"I do remember hearing something about Susan being pregnant but that was it. No one talked about it, and we didn't grow up together. So it's not like I would have seen anything," Janie explained over the phone that evening. I sat on the kitchen couch where so many mornings I had felt simply catatonic looking for answers. Now, at least a few, were coming. "Oh, and you can call me Aunt Janie." *Blink.* I smiled.

Janie herself just missed dying at birth when her mother, Louisa, hemorrhaged to death, at the end of 1945 (not 1946, as the adoption info stated). Janie weighed less than two pounds, and although she survived, the family unit crumbled.

"I went to live with our Aunt Marie in Little Rock, Larry was taken to St. Louis by our father, and Susan stayed with Adele, our grandmother. So we grew up living apart and only began to know each other in adulthood," Janie explained.

Susan, she reported, was alive and well. Thank goodness. Janie told me "She is smart and pretty. And for a 73-year-old woman, she is real good looking." She also told me that Susan never had any other children. I had no idea what to make of that. Did Susan just not want children, period? Me or any others? She and her husband, Donald, had recently celebrated their 40th wedding anniversary.

"Really? When?" I asked casually, doing some tentative math in my head.

"Let's see…a few Saturdays ago," Janie said. "June 22nd."

"You're kidding! June 22nd is my birthday!" I felt like there had to be a deliberate connection there. Susan, who cried when giving me up for adoption, chose to get married on my birthday.

"And that's your grandmother Louisa's birthday!" Janie said.

Here was another interesting date-coincidence, even though the odds were not exactly astronomical. Still, how interesting that I was born the same June day as my grandmother, Louisa, 14 years after she died, and both chose December 12th as a wedding date. I don't believe in reincarnation, but I have never doubted guardian angels. Maybe Louisa found Pat for me because Pat was also born on June 22nd?

"That's a lot of coincidences!" I exclaimed.

"Well, how about this one. When I lived in Little Rock in the early 1970s I tried my hand at being the TV weather girl!" Janie laughed. "It didn't go too well, but it was fun trying. I married a director there and followed him around the country as he took different jobs. We ended up in Boston."

That's where the marriage eventually went something like her first weather job, but Janie maintained a home in Boston near her two grown children and another in Palm Springs where, after a long career as a mortgage broker, she had become a realtor. Thank goodness. Like I said, realtor phone numbers are so easy to find.

The chit-chat, at some point, had to wind down. I sensed from the beginning that Janie held back information about Susan. After all, during our earlier text conversation she'd made a quick exit to lunch, putting our conversation off until now.

"And my bio-mother, can we talk about her?" I asked.

"Well, honey," she said, and I knew from long experience that this was a Southern way of saying get ready for information you might not like,

"I have to tell you. I have had the opportunity to travel the world and have been exposed to all kinds of people and lifestyles. I'm a very liberal Republican," she said. "But my sister, your mother, is not. She doesn't have a liberal bone in her body."

She let that sink in. I figured she'd Googled and found details on my marriage.

"I understand what you're saying. I Googled her also and the only picture I've been able to find is one of her standing in a line to meet someone running for office. A Tea Party candidate." Moreover, Alicia had warned me after finding an on-line petition: *she's a birther, good luck.* I asked naively: What's a birther? Answer: She wants to see Obama's birth certificate. Funny I just wanted to see my own.

"I don't think Susan is going to be very good with your lifestyle. She's very religious and she tends to judge." This statement came across as a subtle warning. "She campaigns for the Tea Party in Arkansas and has very strong political views."

"Will you let her know about me?" I asked. I rarely let politics get in the way of a good relationship—life's too short.

"Let me think about this overnight and decide how I'm going to approach her," Janie said. She assured me that the conversation would take place soon. And she'd put us in touch.

I sat there after we hung up to take it all in. This had been a long fishing trip, and to find a judgmental bio-mom at the end of the hook worried me. But I couldn't stop reeling her in now. I wanted to know this woman, at least a little. I'd like to think that if she gave birth to me she'd at least like to find out that I've had a good life. I'd like to tell her she did the right thing giving me up for adoption. Surely, she had wondered.

The next evening Janie called me with Susan's reaction.

"Are you kidding me?" My eyes widened and I felt sick. "She's *denying* it?!"

23

PARENT-NOIA

I gaped, looking like a fish myself. I find my bio-mother and she denies my existence? I was truly incredulous. "I'll send you a DNA kit, Janie! I swear I'm not lying about any of it!" I felt myself going off in a tailspin. Susan claimed I had *never happened.*

"No, honey, believe me, when you sent that non-id story along after we talked, I read it. And I believe you, sweetheart. And, honestly, I do remember a little talk back then…" she trailed off.

"Really? So you knew?"

"I didn't really *know*, I mean, I was only 14. And, like I said, Susan and I didn't grow up together, so we weren't close. But my aunt who raised me, she was into everyone's business, Susan's included. I just remember her stomping around saying that Susan was pregnant."

"Well, she was," I fumed.

"I know, I know. But honestly, after overhearing that one statement, I never heard anything ever again. And I suspect, I'm just guessing, that she never told Donald about this. She would keep something like this to herself, I just feel certain, and I don't know how he is going to feel about this."

"Then don't pursue it," I said. "I don't want to wreck anyone."

"Well, I think you'd be good for her, she needs to know someone like you—someone to challenge her world a bit," I knew what she meant.

"Okay, I get it. If she doesn't want to know me, then that's okay, it really is. I just want to thank her, that's all—just thank her for what she did for me. She gave me life and I appreciate that, and I am just thankful that she gave me up for adoption. That she didn't abort me or anything."

Aunt Janie had made the initial contact with Susan, which I wanted her to do. Coming from Janie, Susan would know that her sister knew about me and, also, that I had no scam going. Ever since Pat and Jimmy retired they had been winning Spanish Lotteries and been anointed with Nigerian bank accounts, so I was very cognizant that someone who suddenly makes any kind of claim is a little suspect. Janie emailed Susan that a long lost relative had friended them both on Facebook and to accept the request… which Susan did. Then, she spoke directly to her. She told her that her son had re-appeared, as a TV weatherman, in Houston, and (I'm guessing) that I'm a great guy. Aunt Janie let me know that Susan would have none of it.

Aunt Janie explained her first conversation. "She simply isn't accepting that this could really happen, that you could find her. The doctor and the social worker both told her to simply put you out of her mind, because she'd never see you again. And that's what she did. I think she's simply in denial that they could have been so wrong."

"Well, it wasn't easy finding her," I said, thinking back on all the effort that had gone into getting to this point. "But I'm surprised she could believe that it might not *ever* happen."

"She thinks maybe there is an identity mistake, that you have the wrong person."

"I suppose I could, but I really doubt it." Was I the one in denial? After all the effort to find this woman, was it possible I just couldn't face having found the wrong one?

"I mentioned to you that I remember something back in 1960. Trust me, I believe you have the right person. I'm going to talk to her again."

According to Janie, it only took a day for Susan to pass the denial stage. Obviously, I had found her. She felt there was no sense in trying to figure out how it happened, because it did.

"Why in the world would he bring all this up now?" she asked Janie. "They told me that I had to go on with my life and to leave that part behind. I don't know whether to be mad at him or them!" I guess the social worker didn't know much about computers and DNA back in 1960.

She's upset you've found her, Janie wrote me in an email. *As I suspected, she's never told anyone, including her husband Donald, and she's angry. She doesn't know what to do.*

I appreciated that. *Well, look, I don't want to invade her life and cause any problems. She knows who I am and I've found out who she is and that's really enough for me. There's no reason to go any farther.* Although disappointed, I meant this sincerely. I had knocked on the door. If it didn't open, I could be okay with just knowing how I got here.

You might never get to meet her, Frank. She's very worried about what Donald will do if he finds out.

Susan's secret from her husband swirled at the center of the crisis. They had never had children, were strong church members, and social conservatives. Now what? How would an out-of-wedlock baby, suddenly reappearing from the past as an adult, square with the present?

"Susan is a good person, she really is, but this is tough for her," Janie told me when I called her the next night. "She worked her whole life to put herself through school, make her own way, and she took care of our Grannie Adele until the day she died in 1983." Susan had saint traits, no question. "And she doesn't like the fact that you're gay."

Having learned Susan's politics, this was no surprise. But I took it as a good sign: clearly she had been interested enough to Google me—even if she didn't find exactly what she expected. I hadn't known what to expect either. And I didn't know what to do now.

Finally, a week after this whole discovery, Janie emailed me that she had hope.

I gave her your email address and your phone number so I'm going to let it be. She'll have to just do what she wants. Janie had become exasperated with Susan. By this time, my frustration had grown too. Coming this far in my search for the truth to have it all re-buried seemed like such a shame. I thought of my sister Sharon, and the pain she had felt when she got this reaction from her biological father. She had been able to handle it. And I could handle it, stoically. *If she doesn't want to meet me, that's her loss,* I wrote Janie.

She's been watching your news on the Internet, so she isn't just hiding from all of this, Janie emailed me. Being on TV certainly proves an advantage if someone wants to check you out, and Susan's curiosity was starting to get the best of her: What does he look like? Sound like? Act like? Talk like? She had to admit to Janie she found me to be "smart and good looking. He seems like a nice man." But, after all, knowing I was her biological son, she'd have probably reached that conclusion regardless.

Finally, it happened. While I showered, of course.

Through the noise of the water, I faintly heard my cellphone ringing. During the search, I had grown so accustomed to dropping everything to answer a call or read a message that I jumped out all soapy and grabbed a towel. Wet feet skidding on the bathroom floor, I grabbed at the phone and saw the caller ID with an Arkansas area code pop up. It had to be Susan. I had *just missed* the call I'd waited so long to get!

But Susan had tried. Should I call her back? Should I wait for her to call me again? I had to finish showering. I had errands to run. I thought I'd let her try again. But I couldn't wait.

I dressed quickly and called her from my car. And she answered the phone with a true conservative's mantra:

"Shock and awe!" she exclaimed, laughing nervously. "I'm in shock and awe!"

24

RJ

"How did you ever find me?" she asked, her soft Arkansas accent as thick as cheese grits. The question certainly must have haunted her the past week. After all, neither Susan nor Janie or anyone in their direct family had actually taken any DNA tests. Other DNA connections had directed me to the trees, gravestones, marriage records, and death records that led, finally, down the right path.

"Oh, you wouldn't believe," I said. "It's been a very long year," I hardly knew where to begin. I felt an exhausted relief, as if I had just completed a marathon. After a half century, I had not only found my biological mother alive and well, I could also hear her voice. I smiled and shook my head in disbelief that all of this effort had actually paid off.

For the next hour, I sat in my car in the Kroger parking lot, carts and shoppers rattling around me, talking to the woman who brought me into the world. I kept the air conditioning running, battling the hot, muggy morning.

I had always told people I am proudly from a long line of hillbillies and, in fact, I am.

"I grew up very poor," Susan told me. "We were so poor, the poor people called us poor. I picked a lot of cotton growing up, just to have a little money. We ate squirrels when we had to. After my mother died, my life changed. And I watched her die, by the way, when I was only four. She started bleeding and having Janie and, of course, we didn't have a telephone, so I ran down the street to the neighbors, and by the time we got back she was almost gone. I think they just took her to the morgue and never stopped at the hospital. It's a miracle Janie lived.

Susan's senior prom picture, 1959.

"So my mother's death split the family, and I stayed with my grannie, and the other kids went with other family. And all I ever got from the government to help was $15 a month." I did a quick calculation as she talked and realized that in today's money, that's only about $130—an amount Kevin and I might spend on a night out. "So I worked from a young age, but I was smart and did well in school." She moved to Little Rock right after high school graduation and took a job as a bookkeeper. "And then I got myself in trouble."

I had to smirk a little over that. One person's trouble equals another person's entire existence.

"Well, it wasn't trouble for me," I said, "but, as long as you've brought it up, just where did this trouble begin?" I'm not sure what kind of answer I hoped to get.

"At a party. Of course," she laughed. Susan has a gentle laugh. "I don't remember much about it, but I had just moved to Little Rock to start my life, living in a house divided into one-room apartments. I had left the party because of all the smoke—I've always hated smoking—and went outside where this guy started flirting with me. One thing led to another, and, I have to tell you, I didn't even know I was pregnant for five months!"

"You're kidding?" This amazed me. "How could you not know?"

"Well, I never had any morning sickness, for one thing."

"That makes me feel proud, somehow," I said.

"And I kept spotting so everything seemed normal to me. Then I went to my doctor for a regular check up because I'd gotten some kind of shingles or something, and he looked at me and said I'd turned blue down there," she paused to make sure I understood. "Which has something to do with blood flow, and he said he thought I might be pregnant!"

"So what did you do?"

"I got on a bus, scared to death, and went back home to my family doctor. He told me exactly what I was going to do," she spoke matter-of-factly on this point, probably much like the family doctor had been. "He said he would make a phone call and send me to the Crittenden home in Little Rock for unwed mothers, and that I'd have this baby and put it up for adoption and get on with my life. He convinced me in such a way that I thought maybe he'd already picked out a new family for you!" As she revisited these memories, long pushed to the back of her mind, her tone changed, as if she were seeing more details to come into focus as she spoke. "And then, I'll never forget, it was March, and a huge snowstorm had happened, and I had to take that bus back down to Little Rock, slipping everywhere. And, finally, we got into town, and I checked into the Crittenden Home."

"So you considered no other alternatives?" I had always wondered.

"Honestly, Frank, I didn't even know there were any other alternatives. I mean, I was five months along at that point. My doctor just told me what to do, and I did it."

"I actually have information from when you talked to a social worker," I told her, referring to the non-identifying papers. "It sounded like you didn't get along at the Crittenden home."

"Yes, I remember the social worker would come and interview us, and ask us all kinds of questions. Oh, that home was awful. Let me tell you, those girls had little babies with them and were pregnant with more, and they smoked and drank and they just didn't seem to care about what they'd gotten themselves into. I asked to go to a lady's house I'd heard of," she thought a minute, fishing for a name. "Mrs. Wyatt. She would help a few girls, and I was much happier there. She lived close to the hospital."

I asked her about my birthplace, Pulaski State Hospital, the one name I had known all along.

"Oh, no! You weren't born there!" she said. "You weren't born at the state hospital, you were born in St. Vincent's hospital."

"No," I tried to protest. "My birth certificate says Pulaski State Hospital."

"Well, I was there!" She laughed, leaving me mystified. I couldn't figure how such a mistake could have been made on my birth certificate, but it had been. "You weren't easy to deliver, either, by the way."

"Really? What happened?"

"I'm not sure, but you left the placenta and all this other stuff up in me, and they had to go back in later and open me up to get it out before it caused an infection."

"Oh, sorry." How do you respond to that? I tried to joke, "I've always traveled light."

"You know I never got to lay eyes on you or hold you, either, not even once. But I tried. There was another girl I had made friends with, who was in there for the same reason, and she and I tried to sneak up to the maternity ward to see the babies up on the fourth floor. But they caught us just as we got there and made us go back to our room, and then they watched us very carefully after that."

"Did you name me?" I had always wondered what her name for me might have been. And why.

"Ha! I named you after the doctor who delivered you, Raymond Joseph. I just loved him. He was the kindest doctor I'd ever known, and very good looking, so I named you after him." This doctor's name is on my birth certificate, so no doubt about that part. I tried the name on for size and decided immediately I would not want to be Ray or Joe—but I liked RJ. I could be an RJ, I supposed. Guys with initials for names always seemed to be a little cooler than the rest.

No one, including Susan, seems to know what happened to me after the day I was born. My adoption didn't happen until October, so there is a missing four months. We can only assume that foster care held on to me, maybe at the state hospital, which might explain why that hospital's name ended up on my birth certificate. Or maybe I went back to Mrs. Wyatt's. I have heard that those first months of mother/child bonding are important, but I'm proof that it isn't the end of the world if it doesn't happen. Someone, somewhere took good care of me.

"Who was this aunt of yours I read about, the one who called the governor?" I asked.

"Oh, Aunt Marie. She didn't call any governor," Susan chuckled. "She just said she did. She could act a little crazy, always in everyone's business, and I wasn't going to have anything to do with her."

"Do you think she wanted you to keep me?"

"Who knows? She might have wanted to raise you herself. I really could never figure her out. That all happened when her husband happened to be driving down the street and saw me and another girl walking along, and obviously we were both pregnant. So he went back and told her he'd seen me, and then she got all involved. I really didn't want anything to do with her, so I refused to see her." How different my life would have been if the governor *had* stepped in.

Susan had managed to obtain her own birth certificate when she left high school so she could use it as an ID to get a job. Remarkably, it listed the father who'd abandoned her, Mark Harmon. So Susan went by the "Harmon" name at the time of my birth, giving me the same original last name: Raymond Joseph Harmon. I decided that R.J. Harmon would have made a good weatherman's name. "And I wanted my son to know, if he ever wanted to, his mother's name," she added. She must have had some inkling that I might return, despite the fact that I have never seen that birth certificate. I seriously doubt the original even exists.

When I asked her about getting married on June 22nd, the birthday her mother and I shared, she confirmed that it was no coincidence. "It's a date that I always wanted to have meaning," she said.

Years later, in 1973, she met an Air Force man when he accidentally called the wrong phone number. "He liked the sound of my voice and so he called back a day later and he kept calling and we kept talking. Eventually, he talked me into going on a date and we did and a year later we married." I loved this story. Most people meet through friends, or at a place, or perhaps on a subway. Few meet having called the wrong number.

We had been talking some time, and I was still burning gas running the car's air-conditioning, but time didn't matter at this point. I finally felt comfortable enough to ask about Part Two. "What about my father? Do you have any idea who he is?"

"Honestly," Susan said. "I don't remember his name."

"Well, I know it's *Hensley*, does that name at least ring a bell?"

She seemed to mull this over a moment. "Nope, it really doesn't. It could be any name, I think. That was so long ago and I really just put it out of my mind."

"The non-id info says he was 22, brown eyes, brown hair, 5 feet 11 inches and 170 pounds. That he drove a truck."

Nothing came up for her. "I remember him," she assured me, "but just not the name—it's been 50 years!"

"But you had been seeing him for a few months?" I did my best to jog her memory without being pushy.

"I called and told him about being pregnant, and he said you weren't his and hung up." That might explain her reluctance to remember. Perhaps she just wanted to forget. Maybe she felt resentful that he didn't want to have anything to do with me then, so why should he now?

"Just so you know, I'm going to keep looking for him," I told her. "But I can't blame you if you don't want to know anything about him." And I couldn't blame her at all. Thinking about all of this, I gained some sad perspective. Susan's own natural father, Mark Harmon, had taken off before she even arrived on Earth. Her mother, Louisa, died in childbirth. Her stepfather took her brother to another state, while her crazy aunt grabbed her sister and left for another city. The man who impregnated her hung up. And I, the son she gave birth to, had been given away "forever." Most everyone in Susan's life never stuck around. No wonder she didn't want to talk about this to her husband. And when she finally did, he almost left, too.

25

KITCHEN CONFESSIONAL

Before we hung up from that first long call, Susan and I had talked about having a meet n' greet, probably at Aunt Janie's place in Boston, when, maybe, she would tell Donald. You never know, that meeting might have been the end of any relationship between Susan and me. We could have hugged and spoken, then had a big picture-exchange followed by a "Thank you for having me" moment, and then a "Now let's move on separately with our lives. Email me now and then, won't ya?" That seemed plausible, honestly. There would be no need to ever mention me to anyone else.

However, good people have a conscience, and Susan is a good person. Sure, we disagreed politically and her conservative local church guidelines are a bit more stringent than my "do what's right" code of the Universal Life Ministry (founded by a Hensley, by the way!)—yes, I have the plastic card from the Internet, and I like their motto, "we are all children of the same universe." From our first conversation, without much discussion, we basically agreed to disagree, which is what human beings should do, although it is getting more rare these days.

Susan's conscience ate at her from the first phone call. She had a secret, just like many good Southerners do. As the saying goes in the South, "If you don't think there's an alcoholic in your family, then you're it." That seems to hold true for all the off-the-radar traits in human beings. Just fill in the blank. There are secrets in every family, but this secret proved too hard for Susan to keep to herself. She confessed to me that her appetite was off, and she was having difficulty sleeping. She often felt dizzy. She checked her blood pressure with her kit constantly, to the point Donald noticed. She had to tell him.

I encouraged her to be honest with him. Perhaps mistakenly. "He'll understand—he's a guy," I tried to assure her. "Having a child in 1960 was way in the past, and everyone, especially guys, have a past." And now that I had arrived back in the picture, it seemed to me that the sooner she said something, the better.

She waited until after church and their usual lunch run to Cracker Barrel. "I hope you love me, because there is something I've never told you," she said, sitting across the kitchen table from her husband of four decades. "But it's this." She took a deep breath, feeling the room wobble a little and wondering if a dizzy spell was coming on. "Back in 1960, when I first moved to Little Rock, I got pregnant. I had a baby, who I put up for adoption. And now he's found me." She took another deep breath. And waited.

Donald went wide-eyed. And then ballistic. "So what else have you been deceiving me about?!" he demanded, "And what does this guy want!?"

Of course it would have been easier if the whole "baby put up for adoption" saga had been known from the beginning, but the doctors and social workers had all told her to put me out of her mind; that she would never see me again. She believed them. Why wouldn't she? It's not like computers even existed in any real sense back then, much less DNA testing.

"Nothing," she said, trying to soothe him. "He doesn't want anything, just to know me."

"How did he get your DNA?" he demanded.

"He didn't! He got other people's, and then he used genealogy and the Internet." She apologized, "I'm sorry I never told you about him, but

I never expected him to ever be in my life again. It's not like I did anything to make this happen."

"How could you never tell me this? You always said you never had any children! Every time anyone asked if we had children, you said no!" he continued, and then he added an accusation that must have been so painful to her: "You have been lying to everyone!"

"No one ever asked me if I had a child and put them up for adoption! When people ask about children they mean are you raising any, and we weren't. This wasn't a lie," she responded.

"And why weren't we? You said you couldn't have children."

"That's not true. I said I would have a hard time having children. I had to have an operation after this birth that would make it hard for me to carry a child again. But it's not like you and I didn't try; it just never happened," Susan insisted.

Donald quieted down. "So now you have someone in your life. And I don't." He sighed. The next question came softly, "What other secrets are you keeping?"

"None," she promised, shaken. "None. That's it."

Donald, the younger man in their relationship, suddenly realized my age. "He's only ten years younger than me?!"

"Yes," she admitted.

"So he has a wife and kids and everything? A whole family?" he asked.

Susan hesitated. "No. He's gay."

For a long time Donald slept on the recliner in the living room: miffed, hurt, feeling excluded and insulted. Undoubtedly, he'd spent 40 years with a woman about whom he thought he knew everything. This felt like a betrayal; whether she had said nothing trying to protect herself or protect him or protect their marriage, it didn't seem to matter.

Susan and I communicated while this painful scene was unfolding. For her sake, I really hoped Donald could move from anger to acceptance without spending too much time on the steps in-between.

On the evening of September 10th, I had an email from Susan: *You and I must talk tomorrow. All this drama, but it's very important, and we can discuss in the morning. What time will be good for you?*

26

LONG TIME, NO SEE

Meeting Susan on the down low at Aunt Janie's Boston house had seemed like the best idea, until the big confession. That, of course, derailed the plan. Having a private past and not sharing it with a spouse is one thing, but now Susan and I had a present. A clandestine meeting under the guise of her visiting her sister just didn't feel right to either of us.

So Donald was pissed. I can appreciate his torn feelings of being deceived, despite so much time having passed from my birth in 1960 to when they met in 1973. Over the decades, when people had asked if Susan had children, she always said no, which to me seems like the correct response. After all, anyone with that question is really just asking if you have a family and children at home. They aren't asking if you've ever been biologically "with child," regardless of whether you gave up that child or not.

But Donald felt otherwise, and in his mind it seemed she'd always just lied about it. And lying doesn't go over well. He also didn't agree with putting me up for adoption, despite her youth and financial stress. That didn't matter to him. He just simply thought that *good people* kept their children no matter what. Good people figured out how to make it work, one way or another.

"They're not puppies you just drop off in a box," he told Susan.

"I could never have given him a life like he's had—the education his parents gave him and the opportunities he's had. No telling what would have happened if I had kept him. I was 19 years old and didn't even have my own life yet," Susan kept protesting. "The parents who raised him were the best thing for him."

Donald finally and tepidly told Susan, "Go ahead and do what you want. You always do anyway." She could meet me in Boston, or Houston or Little Rock—wherever she chose.

I preempted and planned a trip to Little Rock. I explained to her, "I don't want us to exclude Donald. I don't really understand why he's so upset, but maybe part of it is the feeling of being left out. We all have a secret and he's been excluded. So, no, let's not meet somewhere with just us. We need to include Donald. If he chooses to stay away, that's his choice."

And, I told Susan that Kevin would be coming with me.

"Can't it just be you?" she asked.

"No," I spoke bluntly, with no intention of dancing around this issue. "Kevin has been my strongest supporter in all of this. And, frankly, any relationship that you and I have is going to include him."

Over the years, Pat and Jimmy had treated my relationship with Kevin respectfully, and they very much care about Kevin and Morgan—but on our turf in Houston. They love to visit us, and we always have a terrific time. However, they are unrelenting that when I make the visit to their small Arkansas town, I must come alone. A lot of friends I know would simply refuse—and some couples I know have broken up over such a demand, but I'm not a fan of ultimatums. I have compromised for the sake of our family's peace.

So forging a relationship with Susan and Donald, regardless of how rocky it might start, would not have any hidden beginnings on my end. My husband would be there with me. Once we knew each other, we could determine the best way to get together going forward. Susan seemed to understand that.

We decided on a simple schedule: arrive Saturday around lunch, spend some bio-mom to bio-son time together, and then all four of us have dinner that night. Donald could show or not. Surprisingly, Susan suggested Sunday church.

"How will you explain *that*," I asked. "Really? You're going to bring the son you gave away and his husband to the Church of Christ. I like adventure, but..." Susan laughed and said, "'This is my son, it's complicated.'"

Like we needed any more drama. We respectfully declined.

I couldn't sleep the Friday night before leaving. I tossed and turned. *Who was I about to meet? Had I done the right thing?* Until I unearthed the truth, I always thought my bio-mother could be anybody. I had wondered about this person my whole life, and I knew her a little bit from our conversations. She seemed like a good person, but I was concerned that her husband had never known about me. *Was the meeting going to be good? What if it went really badly?* All the possible scenarios played out in my head, along with thoughts from being a little boy, wondering where I got my blue eyes. All my life I knew so little about my biological past, and what I did know turned out to be completely wrong. Now the blanks just filled in one after the other. Most of them anyway. I'm by nature optimistic and had every confidence this meeting would go just fine. *But what if it didn't?* I tossed some more.

We flew in from Houston. Over the previous two months, the fear of flying I had for decades had waned. For Kevin, it's a fear of needles; for me, simply an irrational phobia probably more about being "in control" than actually flying. Every little bump, every strange noise, set me off. I even knew that when those engines start to roar on the runway, you have 30 seconds to get that plane up in the air or there's going to be a problem. I had ticked off those seconds by my watch every single time.

But once I started to search for family and realized I had some, this fear went away. I can't explain it. It was as if I could take some psychological comfort in knowing who I am and where I came from—and rest easy.

"When does your plane arrive?" Susan had asked. I hoped that meant she would surprise us and meet the plane. Just in case, I had Kevin roll the iPad to catch it on video. As we walked down the long terminal at the Little

Rock airport, I could feel my heart beating faster. After a half century of wondering, I was about to embrace the woman who put me on the earth!

What did she even really look like? Being on TV, I get told all the time that I look different in person. Even the best picture does not show us exactly as we are. I kept looking for Susan based on that one picture of her which had been taken as she stood in a political line wearing jeans and looking Saturday-morning-dumpy—probably just an unfair camera angle.

"Lighting is everything as we get older," I told Kevin when we looked at the picture. It showed Susan with long reddish-blonde hair, just cut and hanging around her enormous bosoms, and wearing an unflattering shirt with a lumberjack vibe. I wondered why, in a world of viral uploads, she hadn't thought to send a simple picture to me, but she didn't. And I hadn't thought to ask. So I really had no idea what she looked like!

When we got beyond security into the general area, my eyes scanned the people who seemed to be waiting for arrivals. I couldn't see anyone who looked remotely like my impression of Susan. Then my gaze fell on—*Donald*! I'd never even seen one picture of him, but I knew it was him by the forced pleasant look on his face. He grinned, pointing to his left.

There she stood, looking just as nervous as me, but nothing like the one picture I had of her! She has a slender figure with shiny, soft gray hair, not even close to blonde or red. Her blue eyes and easy smile lit up the whole airport terminal.

"You're so pretty!" I squealed. "Look at you! Oh my god, we have the same eyes!" Her crystal blue eyes against her soft silver hair gave her a Debbie Reynolds look. But I wouldn't have cared if she had looked exactly like a lumberjack! There is nothing like seeing and holding someone you've tried to frame in your mind your whole life. In that flash of a moment, I realized how many times over my life I had wondered about my biological mother. And over the last months, that curiosity had consumed me. Now the question was put to rest forever.

We kept on with the hugging, and I hugged Donald, too. I just grabbed him around the neck. "Thank you for coming; it means a lot!"

He laughed. "You look just like her."

"One big, happy family, right, Donald?" I tried to keep it all light and show him that this didn't have to be a big deal. And I did really appreciate his showing up. I hugged Susan again and she hugged Kevin and he hugged Donald.

And there we all were: a family reunion of long-lost family.

"You're the only television star we know!" Donald said, laughing. Then he discreetly left to meet some friends, while Susan rode with me and Kevin to the hotel to check in. Kevin said he had work to do, and my biological mother and I went for a long, picture-looking lunch.

Susan had always been the smart girl in the crowd, proven by the Certificate in Business Proficiency she earned during her senior year in high school. Those smarts landed her a job as a bookkeeper with a glass company after graduation. I imagined her looks had helped, too. She moved to the big city and lived for a few weeks with her Aunt Marie.

"That summer of 1959, I moved out into my own apartment, and then, that's when, well, you came along, and things changed," she said.

"What about after I was born?" I asked. "Did you go back home?"

"Only for a little while. I had to get my mind back to normal after what happened. It was pretty traumatic for me," she said. The social worker's interview had indicated a tear or two, but I really hadn't realized just how difficult the whole experience had been for Susan. "Of course, I felt like the town slut," she explained, "like everyone was looking at me. And then the oddest thing happened. A couple not far from where we lived adopted a baby boy. And my family doctor had been so insistent about my giving you up for adoption that I couldn't help wonder if he didn't have a plan in place all along. I couldn't help thinking that baby might be you."

"Wow, that's a coincidence."

"I know. So I just couldn't bear that. I had to get back to Little Rock."

"So you came back here and started your life again?"

"Yes, I started working as a clerk for a glass company, keeping their books and went on to eventually be a mortgage broker," she said proudly.

"I actually know a little about your father and his family," I told her. I explained about the other relation I had found, Barbara Johnson. After I received my non-id information, I had sent it to Barbara and learned even more about her side of the family.

"Well," she said, her eyes widening in surprise, "all I ever knew is that he'd left town for the service and then ended up in another state." Mark

Harmon, the neighborhood kid who had left for the war in 1942 and never returned to Newport, Arkansas. Susan resented being abandoned, no question. A younger brother who had stayed in Newport told her that Mark "owned a supermarket in another state," which meant he had a little money and could have helped her out. Susan shook her head. "He never gave me a dime."

Barbara Johnson had been the key to the Harmon family. Her strong relation as a first cousin-once-removed to me on *23andMe.com* testing had thrown another wrench in the whole search. But after she read my non-adoption id information, she emailed me excitedly: *Your grandfather must be a Harmon—all the Harmon boys moved to California and owned supermarkets, including my father Larry! I was born in Bakersfield where my mother had an affair with Larry. She never wanted to talk about it, but I found out after the man who raised me passed away. Larry had died too, in the eighties, but I found wonderful cousins.*

That all gelled perfectly. Barbara being my first cousin once removed and Susan's first cousin. Their fathers, Mark and Larry, were brothers.

Finally, the Barbara Johnson connection fell into place.

"And guess what?" I told Susan. "Kevin's son, Morgan, is from the same Harmon line from north Mississippi." Morgan's grandmother is into the whole genealogy hobby. "Morgan's seventh great-grandfather and my sixth great-grandfather were brothers, descended from the same Jacob Hermann whose sons landed in America from Germany sometime in the early to mid-1700s." Like so many names, Hermann changed to Harmon and, yep, the stepson I had been raising the last 20 years turned out to be my distant cousin, but cousin nonetheless!

"So we're all related, one way or the other," she laughed. Then she became pensive and took my hand, looking me squarely in the eye. "What I'm afraid of is when we die, I'll go to Heaven and you will go to Hell." She stared at me sincerely and detected the angst in my face. "That's what the Bible says, and I don't want to lose you again."

That shook me up, and I don't mean just the "all gays go to hell" part. I wanted to jump up from the table and leave her alone with a plate of cold fries. But then I saw the angst in her eyes, too. She was truly worried for me. She faced an impossible choice: what her religion ingrained in her versus her fear of losing her son all over again. If I could change, that would fix it. If she could change, that would fix it. If nobody changed, she feared we'd lose each other in death.

We sat frozen, each of us looking into mirror-image blue eyes. I realized that in this whole scenario I had never really lost anything or anyone—in fact, I had *gained* an entire family that loved me, took care of me, and raised me. And my parents, who'd wanted children so badly, they gained me.

Susan was the one who had lost, and she had lost something very important to her: the only child she'd ever had. So over time, she had put that loss and all that went with it into her own psychological box and placed it deep within her own closet of secrets. More dangerous than Pandora's box: Susan's safe held a locked-up secured personal load of all her regrets, hopes, shames, fears, pride—every emotional moment she went through in her own life while giving me mine. Now I had cracked that safe door wide open, and all of her emotions swept out, endangering the very beliefs that had protected her. Yes, she was judging me, but I needed to show her compassion, not resentment.

I finally spoke. "Try not to worry," I said. "I believe God made us all the way we are, and he'll figure out how to get me into Heaven." She tried to smile, but I could tell my philosophy didn't reassure her. We wandered back to the hotel, and I decided the best thing to do at that point was have a glass of wine.

Kevin couldn't help but notice that Susan often gazed at me. Maternal instinct, as I had guessed a while back, just kicks in. She seemed to wonder just how life might have been raising me. Of course, she had answers that she wouldn't have had then: I turned out, so to speak, and it is easy now to think that nurturing and caring for me would have been a walk in the park. Few kids are easy to raise, and while I avoided any major trouble, I'm sure Pat and Jimmy could tell a few tales.

I spent much of our time together noticing characteristics that we shared. Like Susan, I enjoy politics and hearty debate, I have an easy laugh and smile. I am lucky to have Susan's sense of humor and charm; combined with Pat's confidence and never-rest attitude, these qualities have helped me make a television career for more than 35 years. Both of these fine ladies contributed to who I am as a man, no question. But Susan raising me would have presented enormous challenges, especially for someone still raising herself.

Kevin promised her, "You must come visit us in Houston, and we'll have a party and introduce you to our friends."

"I would love that!" she smiled. She looked at me and winked. "Kevin's the kind of guy I'd have gone for in my younger days."

"Great, my biological mother is already trying to steal my man. This really is a Lifetime movie!" I laughed.

We never went back to the subject of Hell. Leaving the weekend on a one-liner brought some relief—I'd had tense moments learning just who this mother of mine turned out to be and what she'd been through. Truthfully, the journey of science and searching brought exciting and exhilarating discoveries. But when those trees, tombstones, and government records moved from black-and-white Internet images to a real person,

Susan, me, and Aunt Janie spending time together, summer 2015.

the experience moved from the cool rationality of my head to the hotter, more tumultuous realm of my heart.

Although we had a good visit, exchanged a great deal of information and had some laughs, discovering how like me—and how different from me—my biological mother was left me exhausted and somewhat confused about how to go forward. Especially since just before Kevin and I had left for this momentous weekend, the leads I had been following about my biological father had paid off. And I was scheduled to meet him (and his second wife, my step-mother?) the next weekend.

How many parents could one man handle?

27

BACK TO THE GENETIC JUNGLE

All I knew about my biological dad from the non-id information was age, description and occupation. Born in 1938, he stood 5 feet 11 inches and weighed 170 pounds. He drove a truck. The Hensley name had been the only clue I had. And, coming from the Y-DNA, it was a huge clue, given the Y is passed directly from father to son. I matched far too many Hensley men to be anything else.

Genealogist Angie Bush had never left John McNeill's family tree. And John willingly helped in the search for my father. He transferred his DNA results from *Ancestry.com* to FTDNA, which could easily be done because both companies use the same chip. That transfer gave us additional matches; but, more importantly, we could also compare John's DNA to everyone else we had so far.

John did not match my X chromosome, so he was most likely *not* on my mother's side. But, we shared 7% of DNA, which, at the time I discovered him, was the very strongest of all my matches.

John put his tree together himself. There were no Garland, Harmon, Jones, Price, or any other of my new maternal names on John's tree. But there were no Hensleys anywhere, either. Nowhere.

I'd spent hours looking at this tree, trying to figure some clue. I had nothing. I called Angie again. "Can you help?" I pleaded.

"You are undoubtedly his first cousin once removed," Angie declared. "You share way too much DNA for that to be a doubt. So your biological father must be a first cousin of John's."

"Here we go again, more first cousins!" I thought. "Another jungle of names and relationships to figure out." Focusing the mysterious mother search on a female first cousin of Bettyjean's had turned out to be completely wrong. Susan, in fact, turned out to be Bettyjean's second cousin, making me a second cousin once removed. My DNA sure could pull a fast one. What I had learned on my maternal side cautioned me against barreling down what might turn out to be the wrong path on my paternal side.

Angie agreed, in her guarded way. She had been down all these roads too many times to fully validate any theory until it was confirmed. "Given there is no X match, and that none of your maternal names are anywhere on John's tree, I think we can safely rule out a mother connection."

"There are no Hensleys, either," I said, repeating what we both knew. That ruled out the father connection. A first cousin with no parental connections: I didn't have a good feeling about this.

"Right, and that might be a problem," Angie admitted. "There may have been an NPE," Angie said, sounding pensive now as well as cautious.

"Remind me what NPE stands for," I asked her. I had heard this acronym before, but now it sounded pessimistic.

"Non-Paternal Event. In other words, the baby is born out of wedlock, and maybe doesn't even know it," she said. Fancy talk for *who's the baby's daddy?*

"Doesn't know it? You mean, the mother is passing the baby off to the dad as being his own?"

"That's one possibility," Angie told me. "But truth be told, she might not really be sure who the father is herself. At the end of the day, it just means that no one knows who the father is for whatever reason. And, of course, that makes identifying anyone practically impossible."

The bottom line remained that not a single Hensley showed up on John's family tree, so my father might not know of his own Hensley heritage. I could see the challenge ahead: I finally had a name, but if my biological father didn't even know his real last name, finding him might just be impossible. And Susan couldn't help. From our conversations, I could tell she honestly remembered nothing. So the search began for a Hensley man who very likely went by another name.

"So what do we do?" I asked Angie.

"I don't think we look at John's mother's side because she was Eastern European—Polish and Czech. Your DNA is strongly northern European: Scotland, Ireland, England. John's father was a full-Scot, and he had two sisters who are John's aunts. One of those aunts could be your grandmother." Angie made her very best assumptions, and this at least narrowed it down a bit. One of the nice features of DNA testing is that you can trace your roots all the way back in time. We all started in Central Africa, "the garden of Eden," and migrated from there. The autosomal DNA tests can tell you where your ancestors came from by percentage, and mine were 80% from the British Isles, 9% from Ireland, and 11% other places.

Angie went on. "One of the aunts, Aunt Charlotte, was born in 1920. So based on her age, it makes sense she could have given birth to your bio father in 1938, matching the 22-year-old father in your information. The other, Aunt Bonnie, did have a child in 1935, but that puts him around 25 at the time. But she could have had *another* child in 1938, perhaps placing him for adoption." That certainly happened, especially during the Great Depression, and it even happens today.

Of course, just to keep it confusing, another option existed: I definitely shared enough DNA to be first cousins once removed with John McNeill, so perhaps *John's* biological last name would prove to be Hensley, and he had no idea of it. If his mother passed him off as a McNeill that would explain why John and I shared so much DNA—me being the first cousin he knew nothing about. And if that were the case then that would be the end of the trail. We'd never find my biological father going that route. This might also explain why John had such a genealogical passion himself—perhaps deep down he questioned his own birth and had just been passed off as a McNeill.

But since that route offered an obvious dead end, we decided to begin by ruling *out* or ruling *in* both his aunts, Charlotte and Bonnie. John wanted to be helpful, and he suggested the more likely candidate to have had a child (maybe my father) out of wedlock would be Bonnie.

She was a bit wild, as I had been told, John wrote me. *Charlotte, on the other hand, never had a man friend of any kind that anyone ever knew of.*

I had told John about the Hensley dilemma, and he had another lead. He sent Angie a 1940 census sheet showing the full roster of St. Vincent's orphanage, in Kansas City, Missouri, a long drive from St. Louis before Interstate 70 was in place. There were 53 children's names, but I didn't have to read the whole list.

The third name down was Michael Hensley, born "about 1936, age 4."

28

CHARLOTTE'S WEB

Although John was leaning toward Bonnie, I decided that since she had a child, I would first look at Charlotte McNeill, who never married and never appeared to be involved with any man (or woman, for that matter). Born in 1920, she would have been 18 in 1938—a reasonable age to have a child. In 1940, according to the census, she still lived at home with her parents in southern Illinois. Her father, James, a coal miner, and mother, Leah, were Scottish immigrants. Could she have gotten pregnant in 1937, lived at home and had a child in 1938?

I don't think that fits, John McNeill wrote me. Charlotte graduated from high school in 1938, and going through a pregnancy her senior year just did not seem to work with the times. She most certainly would have been sent off somewhere. But you can't assume. There are all kinds of scenarios. Perhaps after conceiving a Hensley baby in January of 1937, she didn't start showing as pregnant until late May, stayed hidden away all summer, and had the baby in early September? Perhaps she put the baby up for adoption and returned to school to graduate in 1938. Reasonable.

Charlotte's mother died in 1942, her father in 1947. Sometime in the 1940s, she signed on to become a missionary for the Church of Christ. Her death certificate says that she died of a heart attack in 1985 due to ongoing anorexia nervosa. I had always associated anorexia with younger women, from teenagers to early thirties, but a little research explained that this disease can affect anyone at any age and for a long time. And certainly Charlotte could have been, to some degree, anorexic most of her life.

Angie seemed to think the anorexic condition might explain a lot. "Perhaps such a disease points to a very unwanted pregnancy. *Maybe* Charlotte had been a rape victim and never got beyond it." Angie surmised. "Perhaps she was very young, maybe 15, and had the child as early as 1936 and that is the boy in the St. Vincent's orphanage clear across the state." This seemed to make sense. Such a traumatic experience might well explain her never marrying and even her desire to help others, thus the life-long missionary work.

I added my own speculation. "If she was raped and had a child, maybe this created a self-esteem issue that led to the whole anorexia problem, especially if being what she considered fat reminded her of a horrible pregnancy." In that case, any amount of fat on her body might be emotionally unsettling, leading to her intentionally staying thin. My pop psychology always played a role in these searches. Because I looked for those women who might have given up a child, it proved hard for me not to wonder why they chose that route.

So Charlotte's factors—such as age, living as a teenager through the Great Depression, never having married, and turning to missionary work—all seemed to point to her having given away an unwanted child as much as they didn't. Because, certainly—and I never lost sight of this— many women simply never marry, and many dedicate their life to helping others. Perhaps Charlotte would prove no more than simply that—a young lady who felt a calling to serve God. No rape, no pregnancy, no baby, no emotional crisis. Whatever her reasons, she did not need a man to define her, and she wanted to help others. Period. The anorexia that eventually killed her may have come about due to totally unrelated reasons that were hers and hers alone.

I had to acknowledge the disheartening reality that if the orphaned Michael Hensley or any other Hensley man belonged to Charlotte or Bonnie, then it was very possible that at some point he had been adopted and changed his last name, never even knowing he was a Hensley. If that were the case, it would be impossible to locate him.

Old fears popped up about all the things that could prevent the search from working, but Angie pushed me forward. Although she was normally a rational balance to my creative—and often wishful—storytelling about the names we encountered, she also knew that it was important to keep looking and not bog down.

"We need to rule Aunt Charlotte in or out, one way or another," Angie declared. "And there is only one man who can do that. Bonnie's son."

29

PHIL

---

*H*ello Mr. Shapiro,
*My name is Frank Billingsley....I am a TV weather-
man living in Houston, Texas, and so I just want to
be upfront that I'm not a salesman and this isn't spam.*

*I am sending this email because over the past eight months
I've been exploring DNA, genealogy and ancestry roots. I
have recently located my birth mother and her family line,
her first name is Susan and she lives in Arkansas.*

*I also have a strong paternal connection to John McNeill
of St. Louis and have been in contact with him. We have
compared DNA through the Family Tree DNA company
and he is a first-cousin-once removed. I've learned to assume nothing, but it is "possible" that one of his aunts is
my grandmother. I know from his tree that your mother
was one of those aunts and so, again, it's possible that you
and I are related.*

I wonder if you have any information that might help me in my search to make sense of all this, I would really appreciate it. Thanks for taking time to read this and I look forward to hearing back!

Best regards,
Frank

I heard back from Phil Shapiro, Bonnie's son and Charlotte's nephew, the next day.

Hello Frank,

It was a pleasant surprise to receive your email.

The older I get the more I want to know about my family, so I think I understand your interest.

I am willing to send you any information that is locked up in this old brain. If you have been in touch with John, you may have all the information available. But let's try.

I am the only known son of Bonnie Morris, nee McNeill. She had one sister, Charlotte, who never married, nor to my knowledge had a male friend. Charlotte was a WAC during World War II and then became a missionary with the Church of Christ. She was tragically killed when the rear door of the bus on which she was riding caught the coat hem in the rear door as she was getting off the bus and she never recovered.

If you have more questions, don't hesitate to get back to me. Please share any additional information you have as it might further trigger my memory. I'm also sharing this with my daughter, Linda and son, Greg.

Thank you again for contacting me.
Phil Shapiro

Phil's version of Charlotte's accidental death was much different than the anorexia on her death certificate. Family stories, I noted again, carry different versions of the same truth. His version that she stepped off a bus could be true, and she could have been anorexic, too. Who really knows?

Phil's daughter, Linda, soon became a Facebook friend and shared stories about her grandparents, Bonnie and Joseph Shapiro. Her Grandma Bonnie told her that Grandpa Joseph made his living as a gambler. During his lifetime, according to family stories, he either had a whole lot of money or none at all, depending on how his luck fared at the time. Phil had often shared fond memories with Linda of spending time separately with Joseph and Bonnie. Joseph met Bonnie, at the time in her late teens, while she was working as a singer on a riverboat in the mid-1930s. Of course I romanticized how such a love affair started. Those were the days of the great paddle-wheelers steaming up and down the Mississippi River from New Orleans to St. Louis. Folks danced to the likes of Louis Armstrong's band on the deck below, while on the decks just above—the poker cards shuffled, probably rather quietly. Perhaps Joseph was dealing...

Gambling has long been an issue in the United States and the riverboats of the day were not floating island casinos like today. Gambling had only been legalized in Nevada in 1931, a response to the flailing economy. Cardsharks were not admired, despite what Hollywood may have you believe, and so poker games were, most likely, a backroom passion—even on the riverboats. But make no mistake, riverboats did provide an escape; and, as such, they brewed a lot of passion. By the mid-1930s, Prohibition had been lifted and everyone looked for an escape from the Depression, perhaps into loving arms.

For Bonnie, those loving arms appeared to be Joseph Shapiro's, whose Eastern European Jewish parents had emigrated from Austria in the 1890s. Thirteen years older than Bonnie, Joseph fell into the category of "the older man," and that didn't bother her a bit. After all, Aunt Bonnie had always been John McNeill's candidate to be my grandmother, since she was known in the family to be "worldly."

But I needed more than just family stories and recollections, which already seemed a bit suspect. I needed Phil's DNA! And, I laid it out in my next email:

Hi Phil!

Thanks so much for getting back to me so quickly!

Here is what I do know about my biological father: He was 22 in 1960 (obviously born in 1938) and he was a truck driver. I do not know if that meant a long-haul driver or just delivering goods around town. I know he did have a relationship of six months with my biological mother, who lived in Newport, Arkansas, so he "likely" lived within a couple hundred miles of there if not closer....St. Louis, Memphis, Little Rock. My Y-DNA, which is passed from father to son directly, shows that I am a "Hensley."

So, does that last name, Hensley, ring any bells? Do you recall anyone giving up a son for adoption? Did anyone in the family look totally different from everyone else?

If you are willing to do a DNA sample (no needles, just a cheek swab), I can have that mailed to you and I am willing to foot the cost. Your DNA would prove:

1. *You are my half uncle, which means your mother was my grandmother. She "could" have had a child in 1938, but you might recall that?*
2. *You are my first cousin once removed, like John is, and somehow Charlotte is the best candidate to be my grandmother.*
3. *We share no DNA and, therefore, how I am related so strongly to John McNeill is a can of worms that we will just have to figure out.*
4. *I am more than willing to send the non-id information I have about my adoption if you would like to see that. And I am cc-ing your children on this as I would be concerned if some weatherman out of the blue started asking my dad for his DNA!! Like you, I'm just searching for family connections, nothing more.*

Thanks again for considering!
Frank

Within the day, Phil got back to me:

I am going to take the DNA test for you. I am as curious as anyone.
Just some information about me:

I was born in St. Louis, Mo. in 1935. I am an only child (to my knowl-
edge). My father was Joseph Simon Shapiro and he passed in 1960 of a
coronary at age 56. He had two brothers.

I entered the military in 1954 after graduation from Roseville High
School. Married on July 21, 1957. My daughter was born in April 1959
and my son in July 1961.

I have never heard the name Hensley relative to our family.

How about you? What is your birth date? Have you found any other
connections through the DNA process?

Congratulations on your recent marriage.

I think I'll try for sleep again.

Good night, Phil

I beamed that I finally had a relative congratulating me on my marriage!
However Phil and I were related, he already seemed to accept and like me
with no judgment. Whew!

Kit sent, cheeks swabbed and waiting for the results, I continued a casual pen-pal friendship with Phil. He had met and married his second
wife, Sheila, 10 years before, and they lived the retired life of gardening,
swimming, exploring wineries, and enjoying each other's families. Both
singers, Phil found himself consumed with producing the holiday show for

his 80-member, all-male a capella group. And he knew his way around a good whiskey:

While a good single malt scotch is hard to beat, I enjoy a good wine most every night with dinner. What is your taste in wine? I am only a couple of hours from Napa and Sonoma wine country. My new son and daughter-in-law and two children live in the heart of the Sonoma wine country. We visit frequently. We just had the grandchildren for nine days while their mom and dad had a well-deserved break. I guess I should share that I lost my first wife to cancer 10 years ago and am lucky enough to have found a woman that would love me for who I am. Twice in one lifetime is excellent.

BTW Linda told me on Sunday at my grandson's birthday party that she had contacted you. She is a great person and I am very proud of her. I have been in and around the Education community for 35 years and while I might be somewhat prejudiced I think she is one of the best school teachers that I have had the good fortune to observe.

I do go on! If you and/or Kevin get a chance to get out to San Francisco or Northern CA let us know and we'll make it a great time had by all.

Later,
Phil

I continued my Facebook friendship with Linda, who seemed enthralled with the DNA process. She reached out wanting to test her own DNA, as well. That would be a good idea if for some reason Phil's DNA didn't test well. Not all DNA does. Some samples can be corrupted, which is why it takes so long to analyze it and put it through quality assurance.

Linda made some small talk about being cousins—*welcome to the family*—and seemed genuinely interested in her dad's DNA results and the whole journey I had been on. She is a smart, thoughtful person with an M.Ed., and a passion for written and visual communications. An athletic woman, she also teaches mindfulness and yoga. She's slender, attractive, and charismatic. But Linda's longer face and hazel green eyes, like those of Phil's, looked nothing like mine. I would never, ever, put us in the same room together as even being related, much less close cousins.

"I miss my mother, terribly," Linda told me. "She died of cancer in 2005. It was tough. We were very close. A couple years later Phil married Sheila and I inherited another lovely bonus mother."

We were both nursing broken ankles that summer—mine came from stepping in a hole at Galveston's beach over Fourth of July weekend; and Linda, exactly one month later, had stepped off a curb and broken her ankle in several places.

I just stepped funny in a crack, had a spiral fracture to my fibula, and now I hate to get metal and screws in my ankle. First bone I have ever broken, she wrote. That seemed like such weird kismet to me—neither of us having ever broken a bone in our lives, and now just days before even knowing each other even existed, we both independently crater our ankles. Fortunately for me, I just booted up. No titanium.

There were other interesting similarities.

My Bachelor's Degree is in journalism and philosophy while Linda majored in English lit: I love Shakespeare, everything about his works.

Funny. I replied. *I played Laertes in college.*

We were both married in December of 2012, she to Paul on New Year's Eve. Her love for writing and reading and drawing and exploring the more artsy side of life embodies the kinds of esoteric venues I had always gravitated toward—alone in the Billingsley family. My parents and sister were never much for a Broadway show or museum. None of them traveled much, while I headed somewhere every few months. We didn't judge each other; we were just different.

Linda understood that. Her younger brother Greg finds his soul in Harley Davidsons, playing guitar and fishing boats. They are very different in their interests.

"I'm glad we're related Frank," Linda told me. "However we are."

"We'll know soon enough!" I couldn't wait to see exactly how she fit on my tree.

And then she made a small, yet very telling, observation. "You have his ears."

30

THE BABY'S DADDY

On August 20, 2014, the moment of truth finally came. Or, at least, some truth.

It was a little after seven in the morning, and I had just poured some coffee and gotten comfortable on the sofa to check email. I opened the computer and I saw two subject lines from Morgan Hawthorne:

Phil's results are in!
Check your Family Finder!

This had to be important news.

I went straight to my FTDNA Family Finder page, clicked on the link, and watched as my 900-plus DNA cousins loaded up. Then, a new name registered at the very top of the list and the slider indicating "DNA percentage shared" kept sliding to the right like a hot thermometer: 50% DNA Shared.

PHIL SHAPIRO
Parent/Child | 8/20/2014

The half-Jewish guy with absolutely no clue how this might have happened turns out to be my biological *father?* I had him as the perfect candidate for a first cousin once removed, or maybe a half-uncle.

"Kevin!" I screamed from the kitchen. He came stumbling down the stairs. "The DNA test is back! Can you believe it? My biological father is *Phil!*"

"You're kidding! I thought he was your cousin. What happened to the truck driver?" he asked.

My hands were literally shaking at the computer. With the two-hour time difference from Texas to California, 7:30 in the morning just seemed too early to call, so I fired off an email:

Hi Phil!

Our results posted this morning as parent/child! I am ecstatic! I hope you see the news the same way and look forward to talking with you and meeting in person not too long from now! I promise not to drag you on the Jerry Springer show. I also let Linda in on the news and am very happy to already have a nice friendship going with her. This is exciting! You can teach me how to drink a good scotch.

Best regards!
Frank

Later in the morning I received this:

On the 20th of August I became a new PaPa! How many men at my age get the thrill of having a new son? I am surprised, awed, thrilled and the longer I think about this the better it gets.

We do need to talk, meet, and spend some time getting to know one another. Can you imagine trying to catch up on 53 years of life. Wow! We both have a lot to look forward to. My wife Sheila said, "does this mean that I am a new stepmom. I can't wait to meet him."

Let's both be thinking about how to meet.

Sheila couldn't have been more thrilled at this new addition to their family. "It's like a fairy-tale!" Sheila exclaimed over the phone that afternoon. "I can't wait to see you and Phil together, just to watch the mannerisms! How exciting!" Phil felt the same way.

I never ceased to be surprised at how differently people reacted to DNA testing—both the process and the results. Some people are afraid you are giving your DNA to the government, and they are suspicious. And on the finding side, they have had enough bad experiences with the family they have—why add more drama, they think. But Phil and Sheila's reaction was just what I had longed for in my search.

For the first time since our lengthy correspondence had started, I finally heard the deep, dulcet voice of his: "How wonderful to have another son, and what fun we'll have for the rest of my life!"

I sent an email to these new family members: Phil, Sheila, Linda, Greg, and John McNeill:

At the risk of sounding like Oprah, I feel like I have stumbled onto something that is way bigger than myself and I'm really happy to be a part of it! I look forward to getting to know you all and sharing my life as well. I had the advantage of always knowing that biological family was "out there somewhere" (now I sound like a song), while you didn't have that advantage and so this is a bit of a jolt for you—which really makes your welcome so much more meaningful to me. Please know that my heart is in the right place on all of this and I'm truly honored to be one of your family, at the very least in the DNA sense, and the future has become even more exciting for me!

So love and peace to you all (Namaste to Linda!) and have a wonderful upcoming weekend!

Frank

The whole who-is-the-father scenario played out something like a Shakespearean drama: Phil Shapiro? A Shapiro, *not* a Hensley, at least not that he ever knew. Did Bonnie know, passing him off to Joseph as a Shapiro? Did Joseph know and accept it — or not know, or always wonder? Phil couldn't have known I existed, or did he, but played this whole thing close to his chest? When did he drive a truck? I had a lot of questions.

"No, no truck. I was an Air Force man," Phil insisted. I called him that evening between my weathercasts. "Stationed in Little Rock in the late 1950s." But he had at first insisted that his next line of duty came the summer of 1959, when he transferred overseas. When Phil flew in the Air Force in the early 50s, his assignment had him flying into Pacific typhoons gath-

Phil in his early 20s.

ering weather reconnaissance. Yep, my biological dad flew as an original Hurricane Hunter!

"I got married in 1957 and Linda was born at the air base in Little Rock in 1959," he explained.

The possibility of Phil being my birth father had never made it on my radar. For one thing, he didn't fit Susan's physical description of the man she claimed fathered me, and Phil had never been a truck driver. Plus, he was born in 1935, not 1938. He was too old, too tall, and too married at the time. Phil never said that he couldn't possibly be my birth father. But he never suggested himself as a candidate, either.

"So," I started. "How do you think this might have happened?" Of course, he knew what I meant. I was born between Linda and Greg.

He explained that while he'd left Little Rock that summer he had to return. "I had to go back for a weekend for the process of checking out *officially* from the air base before moving on to the next base," he told me. "Standard in those days." Phil went back alone to do the checking out, and that happened to be a weekend in late September 1959. "I do remember my buddies taking me out for a big goodbye night, and we did find this party going on.

I'm sure I had a few scotches, but I honestly don't remember anything else about that night." I, apparently, turned out to be the party favor.

Linda did not appreciate the humor in this line. She is a kind lovely person with a welcoming and endearing spirit, but, clearly, my being a year younger proved that her father had stepped out on her mother. She obviously felt strong loyalty to her mother. Revering her mother's memory, forgiving her father, finding a place in her heart for a new brother—the emotions she felt all at once were as twisting in her soul like the yoga moves she teaches. Linda demanded a meeting with Phil, and they met for coffee.

I have no direct knowledge of just how they hashed out the past, but I am certainly glad they had the guts to just lay the truth on the table and talk about it. Linda will always tell you the truth, whether you want to hear it or not, and I'm sure she had a few choice words for Phil that day. The discussion seemed to settle them in to the present. Regardless of the circumstances: I exist. And they are both happy about that.

As it would happen, all three of us "kids"—Greg, Linda, and I—have tattoos. And I don't mean crazy, drunken, teenage tattoos.

Phil and I, the first time we met.

We all got inked as adults to camouflage scars from various operations. I am sporting a Snow Leopard on my lower left back where I had a lumbar fusion as a young teenager. Linda's Tinker Bell and flowers camouflage a mastectomy scar and Greg sports a dragon that Linda tattooed on his back to hide a scar. You read about siblings separated at birth and meeting later in life to discover they have amazing similarities—preferring the same toothpaste or sodas or cigarettes. Of all things, I never expected our commonality to be ink.

And Phil and I had another commonality that we couldn't ignore.

31

NUMB & NUMB-ER

O ver the phone, I tried to explain as delicately as I could. "Well, Phil, I had my DNA tested for what they call the Y-DNA, which is for the Y-chromosome and it is passed directly from father to son. I got my Y from you and you got yours from your dad and so on." I let that settle a bit to set the stage. "And that Y-DNA test very strongly indicates that I am a *Hensley*. In fact, all this time I have actually been looking for a man named *Hensley* to be my birth father.

"That's part of what has been so confusing. I couldn't find any Hensleys on any of the family trees I have been searching. But, there are also no Shapiro names from that Y-DNA test. None at all. Or any other Jewish names." I took another pause to see if that would sink in on its own, then I continued. "So if I am *Hensley*, then you are a *Hensley*. I don't know if you ever suspected that, or ever even heard the name mentioned."

He didn't say anything. I thought about the nature of DNA as I had come to understand it, what was just speculation based on certain percentages shared, and what was undeniably true. Based on the DNA, what I was about to tell him was a fact. I couldn't believe my search had brought me to the point of having to deliver news like this. "I mean, I just feel like I have to be honest with you: you are not a Shapiro."

He took a deep breath over the phone, stoically quiet for a moment. Then, in his wonderful baritone voice, he said, "You know, my mother wasn't Jewish, and I wasn't brought up in that faith. But I sat *shiva* for my father when he died, because I felt that's what a son should do for his Jewish father. He's buried in the Mt. Sinai cemetery in St. Louis. In fact, his father before him, my grandfather, kept the Jewish cemetery records there. He emigrated from Hungary in 1897." Phil sighed. "He taught me many lessons as a boy."

Then he went on. He was not as blindsided by this news as I had expected. "My mother and father married in June of 1935, six months before I came along. But I always assumed he'd gotten her pregnant and married her because of it. I really have no idea if he ever realized I might have been another man's son." He paused. "Maybe he knew and accepted that, but he always treated me like his son." And, he said, by all accounts, Joseph Shapiro truly loved Bonnie, too, although she never seemed to feel the same about him. "She would leave for weeks at a time to go sing on those riverboats, and we'd be alone."

"And Joseph made a living as a riverboat gambler?" I asked.

"My mother used to say that, and I never doubted it, but I didn't know him to be much of a gambler or a traveler. He clerked his whole life in a hotel as far as I knew." Part of the mystery is that no one really knew Bonnie's whereabouts in the mid- and late-1930s, or where she lived exactly. She'd be away for months at a time. Riverboat history is well-documented, but the people who worked the boats and the passenger manifests are not so available. Who knows what stories arise when people are protecting their reputations?

On the other hand, Bonnie may have honestly always thought that Joseph did father Phil. After all, my adoption information about my father was clearly wrong, although even my mother thought it to be completely true.

Despite the unconventionality of his parents' relationship, Phil never had any reason to doubt his being a Shapiro by blood and birth. I cannot imagine being 78 years old and suddenly finding out, without asking for it, that you have a son you never knew about, that your father is not your father, and that you have no true Jewish DNA.

As exciting as it was for me to discover Phil was my biological dad, delivering all of that news to Phil left me feeling hollow and a little mean. I felt selfish. Just because I wanted to know who I am, didn't mean he wanted to know who he wasn't. But Phil seemed to take it in stride.

He wrote me an email that evening:

Seems like there is lot to learn about the "family." If what I have read is accurate, my memory makes me think about happenings as a youth that raise more questions than I can answer. One lie begets another. One of the sayings I heard from the men in the Shapiro family is, "you always know who your mother is but you can't always be sure about your father." It was claimed to be an old Yiddish saying. As I talk about my past, the more questions I have. It is amazing how many different directions the mind can go with so little evidence.

What all can you tell me about how you researched finding me? You are the only certainty so far and that lightens my heart. Some mornings all I want to do is get to know you and about you. Other mornings I also want to pursue more. At my age, I want to know all and sometimes nothing.

Since he asked, I replied with another suspicion that I had developed: *You might have a brother.*

32

UNITED STATE

The day I was to meet Phil, Dominique asked. "How are you handling all of this? Emotionally?" I had filled her in on the discoveries of the recent week and the meeting with Susan. Throughout the summer, she had been one of the people I had kept up-to-date about my genealogical sleuthing. I was always focused on putting the clues together, but she had recognized from the beginning that what I was experiencing was a life-changing, cathartic event.

Other people can be so much more objective about our actions and see meaning we don't recognize at the time. I kept insisting, "I'm just trying to find who gave birth to me." But a few good friends like Dominique said, "Hey, wait. This is not a treasure hunt. This will affect lives in a way that you can't even see yet."

In response to her question, I said, "One parent meeting down, one to go!" I laughed. "I'm good, actually. I'm relieved."

In some states it is required to have a meeting with a psychiatrist before you begin a search process for family, and you have to have a certified letter to proceed. Now I believe that people should at least find a support group of some sort, hopefully including a psychologist who can prepare them for what they might find. But until I met Susan and Phil, I was in treasure hunt mode.

Kevin and I stood at Bush Airport baggage claim studying the escalator, the iPad once again at the ready to record my first meeting with Phil and Sheila. The evening rush hour had been remarkably smooth and we arrived just a bit early. But as the minutes ticked by, it seemed they would never appear.

We'd chosen to meet the last weekend in September, exactly 55 years after that fateful party weekend in Little Rock when I had been conceived.

"There's a big fundraiser for prostate cancer that weekend," I had told Phil. "I'm emceeing, and you and Sheila can come as my guests—it's a big wine event, so you'll feel right at home!" It seemed like an appropriate event for him to attend, not only because he enjoyed wine, but also because he is a proton-therapy prostate cancer survivor. He had agreed, and so now, just a week after meeting my biological mother, I now searched the airport terminal for my biological father.

Finally Phil and Sheila appeared. "Welcome to Houston!" I exclaimed. Big hugs ensued, and we headed to the car. I had splurged a little, hiring a limo so we could spend the drive back into town chatting and not worrying over the traffic.

Phil stands 6 feet 2 inches with a full head of now-gray hair, and he sports a goatee. He commands the room with his confidence. After all, he served as the union boss for a state Teachers' Association for 30 years, the largest of its kind, and became by trade a "lawyer without the degree." Anyone who does that for a living has to know his way around the room. He has the gift of gab. Sheila is lovely, too, and she stood just as confidently. She is a charming woman, the kind who understands everyone's truth no matter whether she agrees or not, and—having been a school principal for decades—she can size you up in a matter of seconds. She has the experience of classifying all those kids on the first day of school: Is this one trouble? Not trouble? Heading for trouble? They make a handsome couple.

Over Kevin's homemade linguini carbonara, Phil told us stories about his life, and one in particular opened the door for me to elaborate on my new theory. "The one really odd thing I remember, that I hadn't thought of in a long time, were visits to an orphanage," he said. "I was only four or five, and my mother and her best friend Tillie would take me with them. We'd take the St. Louis trolley to Hodiamont Street, then a bus to the country to a huge, big red brick building with spires." I got excited when I heard this. It would have been St. Vincent's orphanage; had to be. I had Googled it, and that is exactly the way it looks, standing stately and robust just outside St. Louis, no longer an orphanage but a social services center.

He continued. "What I remember most is that they would never take me inside with them. There was a pony ride, and so I'd get to sit on the pony, tethered to a pole. I'd just ride in circles while they went in to..." he paused. "Well, went in to visit whoever they were seeing. I always assumed Tillie had a child there, but I really don't know."

He looked at me directly. "This is what you meant. Could I have had a brother?"

One that looked a lot like him, so Bonnie wouldn't take him inside with her? Could an ongoing riverboat affair with a Hensley man, perhaps the gambler, have produced another child? When Phil had told me earlier that Bonnie would disappear from St. Louis for weeks at a time to sing on the riverboat, I added that information to the name Michael Hensley that appeared on the St. Vincent's orphanage document John McNeill had sent me. I developed the working theory that Bonnie had Phil by a Hensley in late 1935, and then Michael Hensley in late 1936 or even 1937, hiding the pregnancy from Joseph and then putting the boy in the St Vincent's orphanage in Kansas City. After all, the riverboats weren't only on the Mississippi then, but also on the Missouri River sailing from St. Louis to Kansas City. And now Phil's story made me wonder if Bonnie had Michael moved to St. Louis so that she could visit every week.

When I had originally mentioned the possibility of a brother to Phil, I think I had overwhelmed him with new information about his life. He had suggested that we wait until we got together to explore any further. But, now he was asking for more information.

177

"Yes," I said, pouring us all another glass of wine. "That's what I think. Brother, maybe even a twin. That would explain why your mother left you outside—she couldn't have you going in and seeing another child who looked exactly like you!" Phil would never have understood that as a child.

"Oh, wow," he leaned back and seemed to take this all in. "Some kind of Sophie's Choice?"

"Well, it was the Depression. More than one child has been given up out of poverty," I said, thinking of my own situation. "I don't know, but let's face it: Who do you go visit in an orphanage every Sunday if not your own child?" Phil just nodded.

But we had no answers.

Phil recalled Tillie's last name—Spiller with a hard "e" sound. Alicia found her: Tillie Spiller, born in 1913, died in 2001. Her father, like Bonnie's, mined coal and had immigrated from Austria with the last name "Speiler." Tillie is in the 1930 census working as a farm "servant" for the Baker family of Springfield who had a two-year-old son, so apparently she had a job as the modern-day nanny. She is not listed in the 1940 census, but the Bakers *are* listed, running a lumber company in Pasadena, California. So the trail for Tillie ended after the 1930 census, except for the Social Security Index showing her death on October 28, 2001. There was no indication that she ever married or had children.

The next day, I learned more details about Phil's—*my*—family. Bonnie eventually went on to become pregnant by Elwood Hanson in 1946. He was a large man, whom Bonnie found engaging. However, Joseph Shapiro had had enough, and their divorce was finalized that same year. Bonnie married Elwood, and he moved the family to California in 1947. That added more to my twin theory—perhaps by then Michael Hensley, now 10 or 11, had been adopted. The orphanage visits stopped. The family moved far away from St. Louis. Bonnie would have two sons with Elwood. He passed away in 1988 and Bonnie in 1993.

"Those were my two half brothers, and I loved them both very much. I helped raise them. Both of them died when they were only in their 50s," Phil told me. Once again, I noted how non-judgmental Phil was. His mother would disappear and leave him for months at a time, but he loved her as any child loves his mother. And who were we to judge her actions? It was the middle of the Depression, she was a coal-miner's daughter, and most families were just struggling to survive.

––––––––––––

We wrapped up the weekend with a Sunday sip-and-see. Usually, friends are invited to see the newborn baby for that kind of party, not see the new birth parent. I guess you never know these days. Two dozen friends and family had been on this journey with me, always listening intently to this winding DNA story, patiently and probably for far too long. I owed them a drink and at least an introduction to my long lost biological father! By all accounts, everyone found the resemblance pretty amazing and became enchanted by both the Shapiros, who are long on charm.

We'd all gathered in our "family room," which had now taken on a much deeper meaning.

"Thanks for coming today," I raised my voice a bit, tinking a spoon to my wine glass, smiling and swallowing heavily, just a little nervous. I felt overwhelmed. "I'd like to say a little bit."

A few folks seemed to hear the hush from inside, and quickly made their way in from the backyard. The September air in Houston is always sticky until the first front, usually late month, and they probably wanted to jump in the pool. Through the years that pool had brought friends and family together for birthdays, holidays, fundraisers, weddings, dinners, whatever we could muster up to celebrate. But never anything like this. I didn't even know what to call this.

I glanced at the faces of our friends, the ones who had shown a true interest in this adventure, and I prepared to say something pithy, although I didn't quite know what. They had listened in amazement to this story over dinners, drinks, and the KPRC water-cooler as it had unfolded in real-time. These friends had encouraged me over the days and months as more DNA clues trickled in and distant relatives showed up in my family search. They would gasp lightly and lean in, listening to how the branches of my family tree were slowly growing taller and stretching wider. No one, including me, ever guessed I'd get this far in a million years, much less just one.

Kevin had texted these friends a few days earlier—*Please join us on Sunday at our home around 4 pm for a glass of wine and to meet Frank's biological father.* Dominique, Bill, Kevin's former sister-in-law, all our dearest ones: every single one of them promised to show, and they did. Ready to share this moment.

"First, I really appreciate you cheering me on during this past year. I know I went on and on about DNA, which by the way I think stands for Damn Nasty Addiction." They laughed. Kevin wasn't the only one who thought I was getting a little boring when I was researching all the time. "And I made you look at Facebook pictures asking if that guy or this woman or those people looked like me." They chuckled again. "I know, I know. They all look like me, right? Blue eyes, dirty blond hair with a little ginger in it, we gotta be related," I smiled, laughing at myself. I'd gotten to the point where almost everyone on Facebook favored me somehow. "I know I went over the edge sometimes, and I bet it seemed pretty silly, so thanks for not giving up on me!"

I took a sip of wine and smiled. I could feel my cheeks warming and my eyes welling up a little. Deep breath. "I want you to think about your own families for just a moment and then consider this—" I paused. I can be dramatic, but I meant this. "A year ago, I did not know one single, solitary person in this whole world who I could point to and simply say: *That person is my blood relative,*" I shrugged my shoulders and raised my arms, shaking my head a little, to emphasize the emptiness. "Not one. All of you probably take for granted that your mom and dad and brothers and sisters are all your biological family and so you don't even think about it. Your aunts, uncles, cousins, whoever. You are all just related. You all share the same DNA. Even my adopted sister has her own children now who she's blood related to, but not me. I've never had anyone. And that's not to say I don't have you all who love me—that's not the point at all. You don't have to share blood to be family, that's for sure. But until recently I didn't know a single soul I shared any DNA with. That can be a very strange feeling. Honestly, it can be a very alone feeling if you think about it too much."

I could see some of my friends wiping tears off their cheeks with the back of their hand. Others looked very intent. Over this journey a number of them had admitted that their own families had long buried the stories of half siblings they'd never met and fathers they weren't sure about. Everyone seems to have messy ivy clinging to at least a few branches of their family tree. Going out on those limbs requires courage.

I continued, relieved to get the dramatics out of the way and move on to the happy conclusion that brought us all together.

"But that's all changed!" I smiled bigger. "And now in this amazing moment of my life, I most definitely feel like I am part of something much bigger than myself. And I honestly can't believe that this all happened."

Phil and Shiela's first Houston visit.

I took one more deep breath, glancing across the room, landing my focus on Phil. Just like me, he has to watch his salt and can't eat peppers or he'll be sitting on the toilet all night. Just like me, he had to grow into his big ears, and just like me he loves an audience. Just like me, he has met his share of hurricanes head on. And, as if there could be any more coincidences, he had a short-scar face lift two decades ago and I'd had one just four years before—can a penchant for cosmetic surgery *really* be found in a person's DNA? I raised my glass and toasted the man who had, without ever even knowing it, given me half his DNA. Talk about a surprise party.

I raised my glass. "Thank you, Pops." I used the nickname I adopted for him over the weekend. He sat there, nodding with a big smile, listening to what I had to say, putting up with a tiny bit of pain having thrown his back out that very morning. One tiny movement and—bam—lower back pain. We *had* to be related.

"And," I searched out Dominique. "Thank you." I tilted my glass in her direction. She looked at me as if to ask "what for?" but she definitely knew. She broke into her infectious TV smile and sent me a quick wink. After all, if she had never forwarded me that email, we would not have been gathering to celebrate now.

"I tried to deny what a big deal this was," I said, looking at her. "But you knew. This has truly been a life changer—to find all of my biological family, and find them alive and healthy and actually wanting to know me. I've had a lot of help, and I've been especially lucky." I raised my glass. "I am testament that this kind of search can be done and be successful. I thank all of you for sharing it with me! Thank you all, and thank you, Phil, for taking that DNA test when you didn't have to!"

"And you, Phil," my colleague Bill Balleza turned to him. "What do you think about all this?"

He cleared his throat, softly. "I have a new love in my life."

It's all he said. And all he needed to say. And that was the end of the story.

Or so I thought.

33

A WILDE CHILD?

Dear Anonymous,
My name is Frank Billingsley and we have a pretty strong match of DNA showing second cousins or second cousins once removed. I'm adopted and have found pretty much everyone, but am stuck on my father's father—we know his last name: Hensley. I wonder if you have any Hensleys in your tree? Thanks!

Here we went again. Emails to anywhere.

A lot of *23andMe.com* customers aren't looking for family necessarily, but are more interested in just what physical traits have been passed down the line. They submit their DNA solely to compare with others to learn more about their own health, good or bad—everyone who participates takes surveys and, perhaps, finds a gene mutation harboring current traits or future diseases. Genetic research continues to discover markers for what we inherit, literally from A to Z, everything from "Alcohol Flush Reaction" to "Zellwegger Syndrome Spectrum." Consequently, a lot of people on the site list themselves as *Anonymous*; but this anonymous match of mine stood out because of the high percentage of DNA we shared.

The match had shown up just before Thanksgiving, more than a year after Phil and Sheila's visit to Houston. By this time, I had found plenty of cousins through the various testing companies, and I figured out pretty quickly their relationship to me, and where they fit on my family tree. But the Hensley piece that would tell me about Phil's father and possible brother still eluded me. I had plenty of people matching as distant cousins, but the common relatives that we all went back to in the 1700s and early 1800s all had so many children it became hard to know exactly which Hensley went where! Census records really weren't a lot of help for me until 1850, when the family listings started to include the actual names of wives and children rather than just how many were in the male's household.

Anonymous responded the next day:

Hi Frank,

I do have Henslee in my family tree. My Great-Grandfather was Charles Henslee born 1862 in Georgia but then lived in KY and died in CA. His son was Virgil Henslee born 1891 in Louisville, KY. Other male Henslees were Thomas, Joab, Benjamin, Oscar (all born in late 1800's) & Abashai (b.1789) I don't have any other Henslee males born between 1900 and 1915.

Carol

My heart jumped. Who knows why the spelling changed, but the double-e Henslees were back in the game. In my original Y-DNA results, I'd been related to a slew of Hensley men, and only one spelled his name Henslee. Now it looked like the double-e club had me as a member. I swelled with excitement and apprehension. I had been able to trace other fifth to sixth cousins to the Joab and Abashai lines; those were familiar Hensley men. Now, I wondered and shuddered, just how many more Henslees would I have to figure out this time? Even though I had found my bio-mom and dad, the search never seemed to end. After telling Phil that his father wasn't his father, I still felt a responsibility to help him know who he really was.

Faster than a Louisville racehorse, I searched for Charles Henslee to find out he'd been married to a Dutch woman, Laurie, with a rare but well-researched last name: Van Buskirk, meaning *Church in the Woods*. Her ancestors had settled in America in the 1600s. In fact, the first Van Buskirk, Laurens, was born in Denmark in 1625 and died in New Jersey in 1694 and his genealogical line is well-documented. I reached out to Angie Bush.

"What do you think?" I asked Angie, showing her the whole line I'd found.

"Search the trees of your DNA matches to see if you have any cousins, even distant ones, who also have this same Van Buskirk family in their family tree. If you do, then that will indicate you share both Charles Henslee and his wife's Van Buskirk DNA," she advised. "And that's more evidence to narrow you down to being one of Charles and Laurie's descendants, but you will want to be sure that it's the same Van Buskirk family." Success turned out to be an Ancestry click away: I found five Van Buskirk cousins! These cousins were distant, and I wasn't 100% sure they were the same family, but this was a promising lead.

I sent a note off to Carol asking just how many children Charles Henslee and his wife had, especially sons, as it looked like I'd have to be researching all of them. I could only hope there weren't more than a handful.

Frank,

Charles had only the one daughter, my grandmother, and one son, Virgil, who never had any children. His wife became very ill and they moved from Chicago in the 1930s to California where they both later died.

Carol

Finally! Only one son! That made life a bit easier, tackling just one biography, but I immediately started shaking my head: Virgil was the first person I'd come across to be in two different census readings for the same year and one week apart!

He's living with his mother in Louisville in the 1910 census taken in Kentucky and then living with his father in a boarding house in the California 1910 census a week later! I exclaimed to Alicia. *One week later he's in San Francisco!*

Carol helped fill in a few blanks. *His father divorced his mom and moved to California first. Virgil one day told his mother he was going camping and never came back! She never saw him again. My aunt said he went west to become a cowboy!*

Carol and I share 1.63% of DNA, enough to be second cousins once removed. Comparing her DNA to Phil's using *gedmatch.com*, I discovered they share exactly twice that, a little more than 3%, right in the category of second cousins! More evidence that Phil and Carol have the same great-grandparents and Virgil being their only son told me that Virgil would very likely be Phil's grandfather. I asked Carol to test at *Ancestry. com* and then to transfer those results to FTDNA—it would be easy to do and inexpensive, and this way she would be fishing in all the ponds.

Virgil married the first time in 1914 to a woman named Bessie. Their marriage apparently failed before he went to serve in WWI on 1917, as his military card lists his sister in Kentucky as his closest relative. Bessie had left to live with her family in Arizona. No records indicate she ever had any children with Virgil.

Virgil married again in 1919, to Eula Short, and lived in Washington State during the 1920s. An email from Carol filled in some of the gaps: *By 1930 he and Eula, childless, relocated to Chicago before Virgil bought a chicken farm in Riverside, California and moved his ill wife there to take care of her. Eula had a "paralyzing disease," and when she died "all she could do was blink."* Virgil and Eula resided in Chicago in 1935, but lived in California by 1940, so their move to the chicken farm took place sometime during those five years. They, too, never had any children.

I explained all of this to Kevin, who by this point had begun researching his own family tree. Despite the frustrations and the elations he had seen me go through as I searched for Susan and Phil, he got to the point where he didn't want to watch from the sidelines. He had always thought his family descended from the Spanish royal family, but it turns out that he's not even Spanish: his name is French. When he started to realize the mystery and fun of searching for these answers, it made us even closer. Of course, given Kevin's maternal Eastern European roots combined with his dad's long Southern heritage, he'll be digging a long time to figure out all those branches.

"It looks like Virgil must have had a son he never knew about," I said.

"Maybe when he lived in California in that boarding house with his father? A single guy living in San Francisco? Makes a lot of sense," Kevin saw the possibilities.

Alicia sent me her own hunch after taking a closer look at the census records: *I'm so stupid. In Kentucky, Virgil was in his mother's house with two female boarders. Mattie Sherman who was 21 and Grace Hisey who was 19. The census for 1910 with them in it was taken April 20 1910. The 1910 census that shows him with his father in LA was taken on the 26th of April 1910. Virgil's father isn't listed as being in the house in 1910. So maybe Virgil left that year because he got one of the boarders pregnant?*

Sure enough, Virgil's mother had taken in a couple of female boarders, and according to the census, both of them worked in the laundry industry. In the California census, Virgil and his father both claim to be in the laundry industry. So a pretty good assumption is that Virgil not only lived in the same home with girls his own age, he also worked with them. Did a relationship form? Could one of those women be my paternal grandmother? Did Virgil just get the hell out of Dodge? Oscar Wilde's quote came to mind: *It's an odd thing, but anyone who disappears seems to be seen in San Francisco.*

"How do you find Virgil's son?" Kevin asked.

"I probably don't," I stated matter-of-factly with a small shrug. "No documentation, no last name, no family stories. No clues. The only hope is that someone, somewhere, eventually pops up as a DNA match. That's the only way. Just wait for a name."

I'd just about given up when Carol's *Ancestry.com* DNA results came in. And that's when everything changed again.

34

THE FINAL "PEACE"

No Van Buskirks. At least none that we both shared. One of the features on the Ancestry site is to simply see who two people's shared matches are. So if I have a match with someone, I can compare to see if they match people on my maternal or paternal side, and that helps narrow down the relationship, maybe even bring a lead as to where to be looking on the family tree.

I knew that I had Laurie Van Buskirk's DNA, or at least I thought I did, because Carol and I certainly were second cousins once removed, and she knew very well that her great-grandparents were Laurie and Charles Henslee. So, by virtue of being from the same great-grandparents, she would be related to the same Van Buskirks, at least one of them. But none showed up.

I called Angie. "What do you make of this?"

She thought a minute. "Well, let's look at the brothers."

"Virgil didn't have any brothers."

"No, not his, Charles Henslee's brothers."

"They all lived in the 1800s! Charles was born in 1862. How are the brothers going to solve this one? There's no way I could have a grandfather born that long ago!" I was perplexed. But we looked, and like manna from heaven the name showed up: Claude.

Claude Henslee, the baby boy of the family, born 22 years after Charles in 1884 after the family moved to Indiana. Claude's father would die just two years later. And while Charles sought his fortune in Kentucky and California, Claude left Indiana with his new wife and baby girl around 1912 to sell tobacco in good-old-St. Louis, exactly where Phil was conceived. In fact, Claude's baby girl, Virginia Henslee, became a magazine writer (my original college goal) and in the 1940s she married a world-famous bridge player from Mexico, Constant Fua. On paper, she felt like an aunt to me.

"What about the DNA share with Carol?" I asked Angie. That seemed to only point to Phil and Carol as second cousins.

"That's easy," she said. "A 3% share can be found between second cousins, but the same DNA share exists between first cousins twice removed."

"That doesn't sound easy," I laughed. Even after two years of looking at DNA shares and tables of percentages and relationships, I still had to draw a chart:

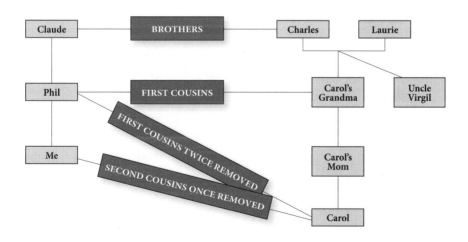

Drawing it simplified it. Claude Henslee, traveling salesman for the new and lucrative St. Louis tobacco industry, would have been 50 years old to Bonnie's 20. Somewhere they met, fell in love, but scandal simmered just below the surface of their relationship. She had fallen in love with a married man. Not the first time for that story.

This may well have explained Bonnie's disappearing for weeks at a time during Phil's boyhood—meeting and traveling with Claude as he sold tobacco state to state across the Midwest. To no one's surprise, we discovered that Claude went into a nursing home the beginning of 1944 and died that March of lung cancer. Coincidentally, or not, Bonnie left Joseph at almost the same time and not long after took off for California with Elwood Hanson.

I found other facts that I took as "proof," although nothing is as convincing as DNA: Claude's WWI draft registry lists him as "tall, dark hair, brown eyes." Phil is exactly that, standing 6'1" and my half brother, Greg, is a whopping 6'4". Phil's early photos show him with a crop of wavy brown hair.

Beyond the physical description, Bonnie seems to have left a final parental clue as to who fathered her son: his full name. I like to think, as my paternal biological grandmother, she's looking down on me and smiling, admiring my tenacity for finally figuring this one out.

I had asked Phil where his middle name, Marion, came from, and he had no idea. "Maybe Bonnie always wanted a daughter," he laughed.

I think I have the answer now. In a final strange coincidence, Bonnie's son's name and her lover's employer's name were the same. Claude spent the better part of his career working for the newly formed *Philip* Morris cigarette company. And before moving to St. Louis, Claude and his wife married and lived in *Marion*, Indiana.

Philip Marion Shapiro.

Hoosier Daddy?

The End

EPILOGUE

If DNA stands for anything, I found it is: Do Not Assume. I made so many wrong assumptions and crazy conclusions while going through my year of searching. Here's one example that could have derailed much of my search: my DNA results with Barbara Johnson showed that we shared the X chromosome and that put her on my mother's side. Sure enough, my mother's father, Mark, and Barbara's father, Larry, were brothers, so she and I are first cousins once removed on my maternal side. Perfect match. However, Mark had a fraternal twin brother, Manny, and his daughter, Janis, also tested her DNA. Janis and I came back as a strong DNA share, yet we did not come back sharing the X chromosome.

I learned the X chromosome can be very particular about the way it gets passed down, depending on generation and recombination. A male can count on the X chromosome to indicate a relationship on his mother's side, but you can't always count on the X being there! Had Barbara's original results showed up without the

X, I would have been searching her side like crazy for my father and would have been doing so in vain. DNA can be tricky, and most experts on the subject will tell you that nothing beats well-researched, documented good old-fashioned genealogy. DNA can confirm relationships, DNA doesn't lie, but DNA does not always connect the dots as perfectly as a pencil and paper. Yep, DNA = Do Not Assume.

I did find my real family and, lucky for me, they are the ones who chose me back in 1960. I took my family for granted. I realize now that Pat and Jimmy, through all the successes and failures in my life, have always been my real parents. Water sometimes is thicker than blood and finding something new by no means replaces something old. All relationships are anchored in history and you can't just blink that. You have to live it.

And when it comes to biological family, I learned that they are "real" people. I had a fantasy of just who my birth mom and birth dad might be, how their lives might have played out, what kind of people they were. Whatever idea I may have had, in reality they are all real people with real lives and families and experiences and opinions. They have had a life, without me, just as I have had mine without them. I certainly found compatibility, but I vowed to myself to go forward making no judgments or assumptions as to who they should be or how they should think. I went in with a determination to love them the way I want to be loved: for who I am, not who others want me to be.

And I learned not everyone wants to know the long, lost me. And it has nothing to do with me. I found my uncle, son of my birth mother's father, alive and well and living south of Sacramento actually not too far from where my birth father lives! He heard I was searching and actually emailed me, and we had a long telephone conversation. He emailed a couple of pictures. He promised to reach out to his two sisters, my aunts. I've yet to hear from them. I know who they are, their names, ages, and where they live. And I am easy to Google. At first I thought they at least owed me one phone call or email – how hard can that be? *Not even a hello?* I had to come to terms with the fact that I simply don't know where other people are in their life, where they've come from, or where they are now. No one owes me anything, and if others are in a place where newfound relatives just simply don't fit in, so be it. Not everyone has to like me. No one owes me a phone call.

My hope and diligence paid off, but not without hours of staring at the computer screen, poring over and over the same family trees, thinking somehow, magically, the answers would appear. I now understand the basics of DNA and how it works, along with intuitive genealogical research. I had to listen to the wise folks on Yahoo adoption forums, from FTDNA and Facebook's DNA Detectives who have the experience of searching and can lead you in the right direction. And I learned my way around *Ancestry.com* and *Familysearch.org* following census records and find-a-grave sites and Social Security death indexes.

I learned patience like I've never known. DNA results take time to come in. Responses to emails took days and even weeks. I friended people on Facebook who still have not answered my friend request. I kept reminding myself that this was my search, not their search, and not everyone would be as interested, kind of like my wedding.

But, I truly enjoyed the journey. From Viking cousins to my biological parents, and I enjoy my relationship with all of them. And what a group! All of us human beings share 99.5% of the exact same DNA—all of us. It's that other half percent that makes us different, but mostly we are all the same. I learned to never let that half percent DNA difference ever become the whole. I learned to celebrate the half-percent differences! After all, I have found Mormon relatives. I have found Jewish relatives. I have found Quakers, Protestants and Atheists. I have found plenty of Irish, Scottish, English, German, Native American, Jamaican American, African American, straight and gay relatives. At the end of the climb, I found my tree.

And I found me. The simple truth. More than satisfying my curiosity about how I got here or where my blue eyes came from, this journey brought me to an understanding of how we are all much more the same than we are different. As much as we might hear that, we don't always believe it. We hide behind sameness without realizing the extent to which we really are the same.

I found me, because I found all of you.

COLONIAL SOUP

Kevin and I visited Phil and Sheila in the Napa Valley, and Sheila made a delicious chili for us. It struck me that "Colonial Soup" actually exists. I encourage you to try it!

Sheila's Chili Recipe

Add or subtract ingredients, depending upon your tastes and quantity you desire. This makes plenty of chili to freeze after you have had a couple of chili meals or throw a Chili "Feed!" This is tasty served with hot corn bread and a green salad (and wine, of course)!

- 1-2 Tbsp olive oil
- 1 medium onion, diced
- 2 cups celery, diced
- 2-3 cloves of garlic, minced
- 1 1/2-2 lbs. ground turkey
- 3-16 oz. jars of chunky salsa (Sheila uses Trader Joe's)

- 1-16 oz. or 28 oz. can diced tomatoes
- 6-16 oz. cans of any combination of beans (pinto, black, garbanzo, kidney, chili, white)

Sauté onion with celery and garlic in the oil until its spirit is slightly broken and flavors are starting to mingle (2-3 minutes). Add ground turkey to this mixture and continue cooking/stirring with spatula until turkey loses its pinkness and is separated into tiny bits. Then add the salsa, tomatoes, and beans to the meat mixture and place the combined ingredients into a soup pot (if you haven't already) to continue simmering on low for a couple of hours. That's it! Enjoy!

ACKNOWLEDGEMENTS

Books don't get written without encouragement and enduring patience from someone in your life and, in my case, I owe my spouse, Kevin Gilliard. He and my stepson, Morgan, witnessed firsthand this unfolding tale of DNA, genealogy, and a lot of luck. As so many people making family searches know all too well, there can be a lot of frustration, and it's always helpful to keep being tugged and nudged a bit.

I also could not have written this book without my parents, who patiently raised me to be the man I am today—complete with a loving upbringing, a fine education, and a stable platform from which to launch, and now share, my life. Their adoption of me, as well as my sister Sharon, led to this remarkable adventure filled with sleuthing and swabbing and extraordinary finds. My folks are my cornerstone and foundation, and I admire and love these two amazing parents endlessly.

I owe a big thanks to my biological parents, as well, for accepting and embracing me when they certainly didn't have to. A lot of people warned me that they might not, as no one reacts the same to surprises or secrets, and what a bolt out of the blue to have me appear on the scene! My biological mother's selfless act in placing me for adoption gave me a life every child deserves. I have discovered half siblings, first cousins, second cousins, distant cousins, aunts, uncles, and a "pedigree" I could have never imagined. I appreciate the efforts of every single person in my lineage who helped me connect the dots. Their efforts were more than words can describe, even in an entire book.

I'm so grateful to FTDNA, *23andMe.com,* and *Ancestry.com* for their powerful DNA-testing resources, which tore the lid off my mysterious gene pool in profound ways. I thank my cousin, Alicia Hall, and Angie Bush, the premier genealogist from Salt Lake City, who are nothing short of brilliant. I would hate to be a contestant against either of them on *Wheel of Fortune*—they are puzzlers. They *will* win!

Developing this book has required months of writing and editing and writing again! My friends Alice Melott and Andy Greenwood both offered advice, and I thank my first editor, Melanie Saxton, for her expertise and insight as I laid out a highly personal, and often complex, manuscript. Every author needs that second pair of eyes, but also a voice of wisdom and guidance, which Melanie provided gently, yet strongly. I also took this book much further than I imagined thanks to Chuck Sambuchino, who became my writing coach and whose editing skills are off the chart. My final editor, Lucy Chambers, really brought it home. She and Bright Sky Press editorial director Lauren Gow, truly believed my story should be shared, and their patience, expertise, and kindness are much appreciated.

Finally, my thanks to the Houston television viewers who have followed my weather forecasts since 1989, first at ABC, and since 1995 at KPRC Channel 2 (NBC). I've been serving a wonderful Houston audience coming up on three decades and, yep, it turns out I'm actually related to more than a few of those faithful viewers. I've had phone calls, emails and even people walking up to me on the street saying "Hey, I tested my DNA and we're related!" Little did they know they've been watching their own cousin reporting the weather all these years!

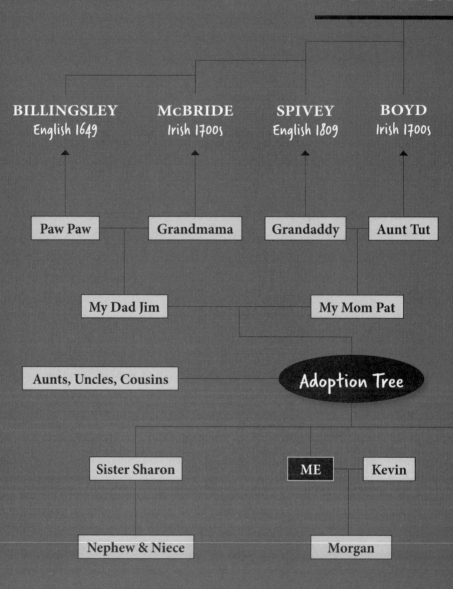

Frank's Family Tree,

ALL BACK TO AFRICA

BILLINGSLEY	McBRIDE	SPIVEY	BOYD
English 1649	Irish 1700s	English 1809	Irish 1700s

Paw Paw — Grandmama

Grandaddy — Aunt Tut

My Dad Jim — My Mom Pat

Aunts, Uncles, Cousins — **Adoption Tree**

Sister Sharon — ME — Kevin

Nephew & Niece — Morgan

Adoptive & Biological

12,000 YEARS AGO

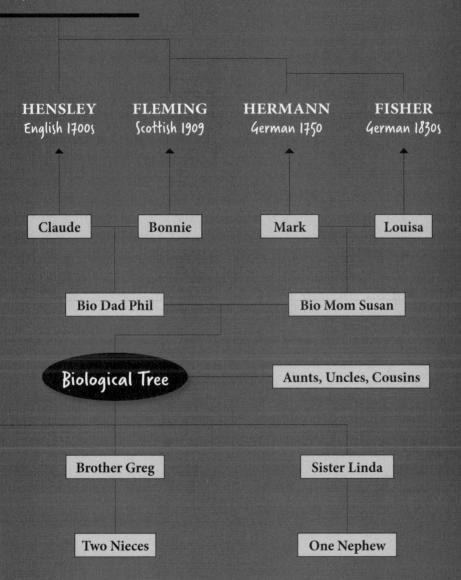

HENSLEY	FLEMING	HERMANN	FISHER
English 1700s	Scottish 1909	German 1750	German 1830s

Claude — Bonnie   Mark — Louisa

Bio Dad Phil — Bio Mom Susan

Biological Tree — Aunts, Uncles, Cousins

Brother Greg   Sister Linda

Two Nieces   One Nephew

ABOUT THE AUTHOR

Photo credit: Al Torres Photography

Frank Billingsley has been a favorite Houston, Texas, television weatherman for almost 30 years, serving as chief meteorologist for KPRC Channel 2 (NBC) since 1995. Born in Little Rock, Arkansas, in 1960, Billingsley was adopted and raised in Mountain Brook, Alabama. He received his Bachelor of Arts in journalism from Washington and Lee University and a certificate of broadcast meteorology from Mississippi State. He began his TV career in 1982 as a meteorologist in Virginia, then moved to Mississippi, and eventually Texas. Billingsley lives in Houston with his husband, Kevin Gilliard, an HR specialist for CompuCom Systems, Inc. They have raised one son, Morgan, who helps run the family fitness club, Quality Life Fitness. *Swabbed & Found* is his first book.

Good luck in your own DNA Family Search!
Visit my website at **www.frankbillingsley.com** for more information.